FEB 0 6 2014

D0289969

The
BOOK
of MEN

THE
BOOK
of MEN

EIGHTY WRITERS ON HOW TO BE A MAN

CURATED BY
COLUM McCANN

AND THE EDITORS OF
ESQUIRE *and* NARRATIVE 4

PICADOR

New York

Glenview Public Library
1930 Glenview Road
Glenview, Illinois 60025

This anthology contains some works of short fiction. All of the characters, organizations, and events portrayed in those works of short fiction are either products of the authors' imaginations or are used fictitiously.

THE BOOK OF MEN. Copyright © 2013 by Narrative 4. All rights reserved. Printed in the United States of America. For information, address Picador, 175 Fifth Avenue, New York, N.Y. 10010.

www.picadorusa.com
www.twitter.com/picadorusa • www.facebook.com/picadorusa
picadorbookroom.tumblr.com

Picador® is a U.S. registered trademark and is used by St. Martin's Press under license from Pan Books Limited.

For book club information, please e-mail marketing@picadorusa.com or visit www.facebook.com/picadorbookclub.

The essays by Chimamanda Ngozi Adichie, Jodi Angel, Gabriel Byrne, Ben Fountain, David Gilbert, Mohsin Hamid, Marlon James, Ayana Mathis, Colum McCann, Téa Obreht, Salman Rushdie, Juan Gabriel Vásquez, Jess Walter, Josh Weil, and John Wray were previously published in *Esquire*, in slightly different forms.

Design by Steven Seighman

Library of Congress Cataloging-in-Publication Data

The book of men : eighty writers on how to be a man / [edited by] Colum McCann, Tyler Cabot, Lisa Consiglio.
     pages cm
  ISBN 978-1-250-04776-2 (pbk.)
  ISBN 978-1-250-04782-3 (e-book)
  1. Men—Conduct of life—Literary collections.   2. Masculinity—Literary collections.   I. McCann, Colum, 1965– editor of compilation.   II. Cabot, Tyler editor of compilation.   III. Consiglio, Lisa editor of compilation.
  PN6071.M387.B77 2013
  808.8'035211—dc23

                                                    2013026356

Picador books may be purchased for educational, business, or promotional use. For information on bulk purchases, please contact Macmillan Corporate and Premium Sales Department at 1-800-221-7945, extension 5442, or write specialmarkets@macmillan.com.

First Edition: November 2013

10 9 8 7 6 5 4 3 2 1

Contents

Introduction   ix

Chimamanda Ngozi Adichie   1
Rabih Alameddine   3
Kurt Andersen   7
Jodi Angel   11
Taylor Antrim   13
M. C. Armstrong   15
Dan Barry   19
Gioconda Belli   23
John Berger   27
Amy Bloom   29
Darrell Bourque   37
John Boyne   41
James Lee Burke   45
Gabriel Byrne   47
Aifric Campbell   49
Ron Carlson   53
Bill Cheng   55
Scott Cheshire   59
Ed Conlon   63
Sloane Crosley   67
Michael Cunningham   69

Contents

Roddy Doyle	75
Jennifer DuBois	79
Geoff Dyer	83
Ben Fountain	85
Assaf Gavron	89
David Gilbert	93
Alex Gilvarry	97
Philip Gourevitch	101
Andrew Sean Greer	105
Mohsin Hamid	107
Adam Haslett	109
Alan Heathcock	111
Aleksandar Hemon	115
Joe Henry	119
Khaled Hosseini	121
Bronwen Hruska	125
Marlon James	129
Bret Anthony Johnston	133
Randall Kenan	137
Etgar Keret	141
William Kittredge	143
Nick Laird	147
Elinor Lipman	149
Vanessa Manko	153
Ayana Mathis	155
Colum McCann	159
Ian McEwan	163
Patrick McGrath	167
Jon McGregor	171
Antonio Monda	175
Robert Mooney	177
Liz Moore	181
Dina Nayeri	185

Contents |

Téa Obreht   189
Edna O'Brien   191
Joseph O'Connor   193
Mary O'Malley   197
Michael Parker   201
Benjamin Percy   203
Jason Porter   205
Ron Rash   207
Salman Rushdie   211
John Burnham Schwartz   215
Mona Simpson   217
Jessica Soffer   219
Rob Spillman   223
Matt Sumell   225
Manil Suri   227
Daniel Torday   231
Monique Truong   235
Luis Alberto Urrea   239
Juan Gabriel Vásquez   241
Daniel Wallace   243
Jess Walter   245
Josh Weil   249
Terry Tempest Williams   253
John Wray   255
Tiphanie Yanique   257
Mario Alberto Zambrano   261

About the Editors   265
About *Esquire*   267
About Narrative 4   269

Introduction

Since its founding eighty years ago, *Esquire* has sought to show-case the kind of inspiring and arresting writing that can shift a worldview or instigate a reckoning. These are stories that entertain as much as they compel, from Ernest Hemingway and F. Scott Fitzgerald in the magazine's earliest days to Tom Wolfe, Truman Capote, and Norman Mailer in the mid-twentieth century to Tom Junod, Stephen King, and Adam Johnson today.

Just as essentially, the magazine has always sought to instruct. Men need guidance on the small things: how to make an old-fashioned, the best way to negotiate a raise, how to buy a suit. But also on the more elemental questions, such as what it means to be a man and how to live up to that responsibility.

So when we were asked by Narrative 4 to help launch its global storytelling nonprofit, we wondered whether this might be an opportunity to bridge these two missions. A crazy idea born in a bar became an ambitious query sent to writers around the globe, became a collection of eighty original stories (in honor of *Esquire*'s eightieth anniversary), became the book in your hand (the sale of which, in turn, earns a royalty for Narrative 4).

Each of the stories in this collection scratches at an essential question: What is a man? For Salman Rushdie, the answer comes from the white wolves in the trees. Ben Fountain finds it in copper crevices of the Statue of Liberty. Two young, dauntless women search outside and within—Téa Obreht in the deserted woods where men wander, Ayana Mathis at the strip club where they drink away their pasts. The monstrously gifted—and prolific—John Berger finds it in an egg, Amy Bloom at the end of a trumpet.

The eighty stories in this collection are sometimes funny and other times soaked in regret. They are about fear and love, ambition and lust, laughter and sex. They are about what it means to be a man today. These stories fulfill not just *Esquire*'s charge but Narrative 4's—to use storytelling as a means to understand ourselves and one another.

Tyler Cabot, *Esquire* Fiction Editor
June 2013

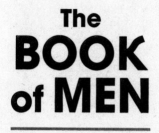

The
BOOK
of MEN

Chimamanda Ngozi Adichie

Our Sundays always tasted like peppers that flared hot in the rice and soups and stews. We sat in the kitchen, knees fresh from pews, and watched our houseboy pounding them in pairs. He held the phallic pestle—thump thump thump—while we coughed and spluttered with watery eyes. Nobody tastes them raw, it wasn't wise. But we did, and then we'd shout and jump to the fridge for ice.

My mom sang an Igbo song about strong women. It wasn't too trite, but it told of places she didn't know, streams, goddesses, women who couldn't read. Women like that would squeeze peppers, I heard, and force them between their daughters' legs—"so they'll stop following boys." But Eros was good for sons. No peppers to curb sons' paths to manhood.

Nigerian author CHIMAMANDA NGOZI ADICHIE, who received a 2008 MacArthur Fellowship, is the author of *Purple Hibiscus, Half of a Yellow Sun,* and most recently, *Americanah.*

Rabih Alameddine

The beating of your heart kept me awake last night. For months after you died I kept seeing you everywhere, hearing you, your voice, sonorous, throaty, reverberating in my ear. I wasn't crazy, I knew you were dead, I buried you after all, I mean, I burned you, cremation was what they called it. But I kept seeing you, doing dishes in the kitchen with your back to me, I'd call your name as you stacked each plate in our plastic dish rack but you didn't look back and then you were gone in a flash and I was left with nothing, not even an afterimage. I didn't mistake you for anybody, I never saw you in a crowd, thinking someone else was you, no, it was never like that. I would never mistake you. I saw you in the hallway, in our hallway, under the Turkish lamp we brought back from Istanbul when we were there so long ago, must have been 1987, before the virus began to scour us. The disease killed so much within us. While I was alive I loved you while you were alive and I love you now but I forgot for a while. Forgive me, I couldn't go on obsessing about you all the time so you disappeared or hid deep in my lakes, as if I bleached my memory, but you came back, you know, like a fungal infection, remember thrush, the furry white stains that attacked your tongue and we couldn't get rid of them and you hated it and I hated it and you wanted it over. You'd been gone for decades, why now, why infect my dreams now? What flood was this? I was buying groceries yesterday morning where a young Third Worlder mopped the floor, back and forth, back and forth, around a yellow sign that announced PISO MOJADO, the mephitic aroma of disinfectant assaulted my senses, and you jumped the levee of my memory, I thought of you right then. Proust might have had his madeleine, but bleach was all ours, my darling, all ours. The tomatoes didn't look too good and I just went home. I'd been a coward, I was scared, do notice I said scared and not frightened, you taught me the difference, you said, Children get scared, men might feel afraid, might even feel terror, but men don't get scared. I'd been so lonely since you died and left me, you left me roofless in a downpour. You gripped the bedrail when you left and I had to pry your fingers one by one, it took fifty-seven minutes because my hands were shaking so much, did you know that? You sincerely believed that the distance between you and me would one day disappear. You told me I was not my father and you were not him either, but how could we not be, how could we not be? You held out your arms and said, Join me, but I couldn't, and you said, Let me love you, and I couldn't because you wanted so to be so close, and you held out the fireman's net and said, Jump, and I couldn't, I felt the fall was much too great, I chose to go back into the fire because that was what men did. I could hardly bear the beauty of you. You said, I liked it when you doze on my chest, but I said, The hair on your chest irritated my cheeks and made it difficult to sleep. You were gone for so long and I moved along and everyone told me I was alive, but last night, in my bed, each time my ear touched the single pillow I heard the beating of your heart once more. Once more, please. Once more. Once more. Once more. My heart is restless until it rests in thee.

Lebanese writer and painter RABIH ALAMEDDINE is the author of *Koolaids*; *I, the Divine*; and most recently, *An Unnecessary Woman*.

Kurt Andersen

More than any other church in Lincoln, St. Mary's was a building people tended to treat as a public space, a general assembly spot for events that weren't christenings, weddings or funerals. That's because it was big and old and downtown, right across K Street from the Nebraska state capitol; because it didn't serve liquor, so you could bring the kids; and because it was Catholic, which in the middle of the twentieth century made it a kind of Switzerland for Protestants—made Lutherans and Methodists and Presbyterians and Baptists more comfortable than they might've been at a Protestant church of a denomination not their own. Thus Lincolnites of all kinds would gather in St. Mary's basement to play bingo, listen to polka bands, watch ventriloquists, whatever.

The day after Thanksgiving in 1952, St. Mary's put on a macaroni buffet dinner and variety show, $1.50 a ticket. It sold out. The main attraction was an actual celebrity, a young guy who'd hosted his own afternoon TV show up in Omaha for a couple of years since graduating from the University of Nebraska.

Kids made up half the audience, including exactly one who'd come all by himself, a wiry little sixteen-year-old radiating eagerness as he rushed to get a chair in the front row. A few months earlier, this boy had won the Best New Performer award at the national magicians' convention in St. Louis. The guy about to appear onstage was pretty much exactly the man he wanted to become. A Nebraskan who'd graduated from college and was plainly on his way to a coast; a *funny* magician; and a *TV star,* local TV, but still. Plus—whoa!—the mimeographed program said he'd been a champion boxer in the Navy during the war; the kid, a Lincoln High junior people called Dick, was a gymnastics star.

As he settled in, preparing to take notes, he didn't notice the boy three chairs away in the front row, a Lincoln High freshman on a rare night out with his big family, celebrating his fourteenth birthday. They were up front because poor Charlie, in addition to his bowed legs and funny way of pronouncing *S,* had terrible nearsightedness.

Charlie glared at the twerp upperclassman he recognized from the school gym, saw his notebook and ballpoint, and thought, *Fuckin' Gallant:* a popular girl in his class this fall had started calling Charlie Goofus, the bad boy opposite to goody-goody Gallant in the *Highlights for Children* comic strip. The show began, and when the Omaha TV guy bounced onstage, Charlie sort of hated him, and envied his easy smile, his natural cool, and his fame.

Another kid named Richard, a sixth grader, was in the fourth row with his parents and little brother and sister. His mom had organized the outing: she worked across the street for the state health department and had been a local celebrity herself, before the kids came along, playing on a semi-pro women's championship softball team three years running. Little Dicky, intelligent but literal-minded and suspicious, was frowning as usual: he didn't get the joke the entertainer had just told about Adlai Stevenson losing the presidential election three weeks earlier, or understand why his dad, a federal bureaucrat who'd voted for Stevenson, was laughing out loud.

Laughing even harder were four people sitting together in the sixth row: the former state attorney general, his former–social worker wife, and their twenty-four-year-old lawyer son, Ted, back home from Washington, D.C., for the holiday weekend with his wife. The father, still chuckling, whispered to his son—asked if he'd ever seen Carson perform when they were at the university together, to which Ted answered no, but that he reminded him a little of his new boss, the freshman senator from Massachusetts.

The biggest, squawkiest laugh at the political joke came from near the back of the room, from another recent University of Nebraska graduate, another son of a maverick Nebraska Republican politician, another young up-and-comer who'd spent time on the East Coast trying to make his mark. He worked as a stockbroker for his dad in Omaha, but he'd recently bought a gas station as an investment and had driven down to Lincoln for the night to look at another small business that a college friend, a member of the St. Mary's congregation, wanted him to go in on. He didn't drink, and the prospect of such a cheap night on the town—"Dinner and a show for a *buck and a half*?"—had been irresistible.

In other words, of the 10,287 males between the ages of six and twenty-seven in Lincoln, Nebraska, that night in 1952, thirty-seven were in the basement of St. Mary's Catholic Church, full of macaroni and Jell-O salad, laughing and applauding at jokes and tricks. And six of those thirty-seven became famous men. Which is to say, the magician and comedian/talk-show host Johnny Carson was onstage performing for the magician and future comedian/talk-show host Dick Cavett; Charles Starkweather, the future mass murderer; Dick Cheney, the future vice-president of the United States; Theodore Sorensen, the future special counselor and speechwriter to President Kennedy; and Warren Buffet, the future billionaire.

And the magic show was excellent.

Kurt Andersen, the host and co-creator of *Studio 360*, is the author of *Heyday, Turn of the Century,* and most recently, *True Believers.*

Jodi Angel

By chance we caught him flat-footed, jumped him in the park. We were drunk as fuck in my father's Chevy; Richie's gap-toothed girlfriend in the backseat bitching that Bobby couldn't steal her dog just because they busted up.

"That's Bobby," she shouted. "With my fucking dog."

Bobby was crying even before I got the bat.

Later, in the backseat, Richie's gap-toothed girlfriend underneath me grinding hard-angled hips, she whispered, "That wasn't my dog."

I covered her mouth with my hand.

JODI ANGEL is the author of the short story collection *You Only Get Letters from Jail.*

Taylor Antrim

The guy came at her with a chef's knife. She shot him in the face. Perfect, I thought, returning the decade-old news clips to her underwear drawer. Because I'm done with nice girls. Because I feel guilty all the time.

I'm not sorry, she likes to say. Which—let me tell you: Makes me want to wrap her up.

She hooks a finger in my belt loop when she wants to get down. She forms plans of her own three nights a week. She has this puppy that she loves so much more than she'll love any human being, ever.

She was drunk on the night in question, but no charges. Self-defense. *I'm not sorry.* I can't say it the way she does.

I find her watching war coverage. Fallujah. Tal Afar. Casualty reports. Guys my age. I say, Krista. *Krista.*

I know you know, she tells me over dinner. And because I'm on my third beer and have no way of covering even half the check, I try a stupid joke. I hold up my hands. *Don't shoot.*

She's cool about it though. Sips her club soda, fixes me with those slate-blue eyes, makes me feel younger and even more broke than I am.

It is just part-time clerical work at a real estate firm, but I commit a filing mistake and try Krista's line on my boss and that's basically that.

Is it her fault? I whisper the question into an empty room. I turn her TV on and it's CNN. Buzz-cut dudes with wraparound shades playing *Halo* in a desert camp.

I deserve an explanation, I say when she gets home.

She drops her keys on the table. The puppy, who I haven't walked, is leaping into the air.

She takes me seriously, which is more than my bluster deserves.

It was his gun, she says.

The puppy is turning circles by the door. I make a show of being unsatisfied, thinking: *There are at least six girls in town I should apologize to. Plus my old teachers, my coach at Westside. My boss. Mom. Dad.*

I used to think it made me who I am, this wanting to apologize.

I move out. I get a job running the register at the Quik Mart. The Navy recruitment office is right next door. The posters are like celestial beacons. FIND YOUR MISSION. YOUR PATH STARTS HERE. STEP UP.

I do the unforgivable thing. I take the puppy. I want *her* to tell me how to act, what to do, how to be. Because the puppy loves me.

No—not me, I realize. She curls and cuddles and methodically licks my hand. She loves the man standing here.

TAYLOR ANTRIM is a senior editor at *Vogue* and the author of *The Headmaster Ritual*.

M. C. Armstrong

I t was the hottest summer on record, the streets of August usually empty for fear of the heat. But as he traveled north on Haifa, Faris saw a mess up ahead on the bridge, a cluster of buses, the scorched faces of beggars and protesters. To his right was the swampy crawl and the dead fish steam of the Tigris River, or what was left of it. Across the bridge was the Palestine Hotel where President Hussein was scheduled to give her speech in an hour.

"Suicide just selling a soda out here," said Donovan Hunt from the backseat.

"Out there, you mean," said Faris.

Hunt tapped at the tinted window with his wedding ring. "Right," he said. "Out there."

Hunt was what you call a cold fish, a forty-year-old businessman with a dark mustache and extremely white teeth, the sort of guy who gave you the impression he wanted you to know that not only was his smile the product of money, but so was everything else, so you'd better get on board if you wanted to keep his valuable attention. Hunt wasn't Faris's favorite client, but he was far from unusual. Hunt worked for the investment firm Mitchell Wesson. His life was driven by money. In other words: a typical American man.

Faris turned right onto the bridge, took a deep frustrated breath, and came to a stop. This is the story of heat. When the weather is hot, most people take to the shade. But still, even that late in the game, one could still see the few who cared, the ones who greet heat with heat, the protesters lining the bridge, the children of the revolution in their tattoos and bandannas, American flags burning like semaphores for the stalled traffic, one woman wearing a black bra and a red hijab with a sign that read:

I AM PALESTINE.

"How do they keep getting a boner for the same old story?"

Twenty years earlier, Faris might have thrown his hands off the wheel and argued his way to the bottom of the Tigris with Donovan Hunt. But that was then. A protester slammed a hand against his door, the contact sending an automatic photo to our database.

Faris radioed in:

"Six eight eleven," he said.

This was a coded message, a request for an alternate route for the drive home. Such requests were encrypted for a simple reason: We did not wish to worry the client.

"Hey," Hunt said. "Let's go to Skyhorse for dinner."

Skyhorse was the most decadent gentlemen's club in Baghdad. There were choose-your-own-adventure game rooms. There were rooms with men, rooms with women.

"Need me a Baghdad massage," Hunt said. "My third leg is killing me."

All of a sudden a young girl with spiked hair and a shredded burka poured fluid all over her body, as if a wet T-shirt for the eyes of Hunt, only it wasn't water that revealed her features.

She lit a match to a dollar.

Rarely do you see these people light their faces first. But maybe for the deeply intentioned, this evasion is not about fear so much as effect, for if the anguish of the face can be preserved, then perhaps the symbolic act can maintain a humanity right until the end. She took the burning bill to the hem of her burka.

"Jesus!" Hunt said.

There are photos of Chou Lin, the photographer, capturing everything, which, to me, is the real picture, these men who take pictures of people dying.

Faris jumped out of the car, removed his coat, and gave chase, spun the burning girl around in a moment that would later strike him as something like a dance, the mad pirouette of the doomsday prophetess suddenly a duet in which he felt the heat of her anger bloom in his coat. He wrapped his arms around her, felt the strange shiver of her life while Hunt remained in the car, muttering:

"You kidding me?"

The traffic jam was now a life-or-death situation. They needed to get this woman to Ibn Al Bitar, the hospital. When an extremely dark African with a gray poodle in a BabyBjörn pulled up on a purple scooter, Faris left his ruined jacket on the road, placed the girl on the back, and screamed "*It-har-rak!*"

MOVE!

He would later wonder whether he'd done the right thing, whether perhaps it might not have been better to let the burning girl follow her urge to send a fiery message to the world. But as he toweled himself off in the cool cabin of the company car, he felt calm, like it was best to leave "later" to the others, to men like Donovan Hunt.

M. C. ARMSTRONG, a former war reporter in Iraq, is the winner of a Pushcart Prize in fiction. He's at work on his first novel.

Dan Barry

He asked again, raising his voice as he lowered his glass. Not good. You wanted that glass of amber occupying his mouth, always.

"Who did this to you?" He muted less urgent news with the press of a thumb. "Goddammit."

"You don't understand," I said.

Misunderstandings were the understanding of the house. And here I was, his thirteen-year-old son, sniffing once again to stop the escape of red. Puffy eyelid. Scraped forehead. White parochial school shirt dyed grass, mud, and blood. Narrow-shouldered too, but that was a constant.

This time, though, the stinging cut inside my cheek tasted salty and wild, like that first burst of sea breath after a wave slam at Cedar Overlook beach.

My gaze shifted between my father and the Rembrandt print on the wall behind him, bought at the Sears on Sunrise Highway because no one, goddammit, was going to say the Tierneys didn't have class. The print was *Man in a Golden Helmet,* the don't-mess-with-me soldier, hanging in that spot for years. Only now did I grasp this art of war.

"You don't understand," I repeated. "I won."

I won.

My father's eyes did an optical jig. He took a swallow you could hear.

"Who's the kid?"

"Ea—," I began to say. "Ronald Kapinski."

He nodded. "Father's a lawyer or something," said my own, who was neither. "Name's on a building near the Arby's," he said. Then, with effect: "Walter. J. Kapinski."

"Yeah, I guess."

"He bigger than you?" he asked.

"I'm taller," I said. "But he weighs more."

"Tell me what happened," he said, repositioning his ass, while my mother stood beside his cloth-frayed armchair, her only movement the slow, rising weave of her Virginia Slims blue. She was holding some ice in a dish towel that drooped like a lumpy boxing bag.

For my eye, I figured, but I wanted to see all while telling my epic. My audience knew the bully prologue: I had been in fights before, fights I had never won. Until now. So I told them.

I'm getting off the bus like always. Then bam. Kapinski jumps me from behind. Old Stump the bus driver's screaming Get off, get off. We fall out and he folds the doors. Drives away. Kapinski's on top of me. He's crying and yelling crazy stuff, swinging his fists. Everyone's watching. We roll off Mrs. Funaro's lawn onto the street. Then I get on top of him. But he won't stop. So I keep hitting him until he does. I get up and he runs toward Grand Boulevard. Screaming and crying. Crying a lot.

"Show me your hands," my father said. I hadn't seen him this invested since Watergate, and I was ten, and the sons-of-bitches in power were finally getting theirs. He grabbed my right wrist, his factory-rough grip cold from the glass. He nodded in recognition at the raw-red knuckles; the scraped flesh.

Then my mother hard-clapped the towel over my swollen eye.

She poured my father a fresh one and said that she and I had a quick errand to run, which was news to me. I threw the melting ice bag in the sink and swaggered out the door.

She rattled the key into the ignition, but didn't turn it. She looked to my corner of car darkness. "Tell me again."

I repeated my heroic epic, verbatim. But she knew.

My father wouldn't. He wouldn't know Ronald Kapinski from Barry Manilow. But she would, from birthday parties, CYO games, and, most of all, my younger tales of the Darwinian schoolyard. How kids mocked Ronald and his jutting ears. Ronald can you tuck those ears in? Hey Ronald can you hear this? THIS? THIS!?!?! Relentless. Jabbing until death. Hey Ronald, hey Dumbo, hey Ears.

Ears Kapinski. Ears.

"Why did this poor boy attack you?"

A shrug and a "Dunno."

"Why?"

"I," I said. "I called him a name."

"What?"

"Ears."

Nodding, she turned the key at last. "Where are we going?" I asked, my voice higher now. No answer. Only the tick-tick-tick of the directional, right at the light.

We pulled to a stop in front of a red-and-white split-level on Grand Boulevard, and I said No way. No way. "No way," I cried, until my closed eye leaked. "I can't."

A streetlight's beam cut a noirish slant across my mother's face. Through the wet blur of then and now, I see her: pretty like a shiny stone in the beach sand, dark brown hair short and sensible, taking it because she had vowed, my buffer, dead at sixty. Studying me. Measuring me.

"Can't," I said once more. "Please."

She reached past me and opened the passenger door. This, then, is how we are formed. I walked heavy-footed up the path, scraped hands holstered in my pockets.

———

DAN BARRY, who writes the "This Land" column for *The New York Times,* is the author of three books, most recently *Bottom of the 33rd: Hope, Redemption, and Baseball's Longest Game.*

Gioconda Belli

The toughest thing for me when I came back as a man was to get used to the dangling thing between my legs. I had come back before as a dog, then as a cat, then as a parrot. I kept wishing for the day when I would come back as a human being. I had been a woman the first time. But being a man requires a lot of muscle. Literally. I didn't think so while I was growing up. I felt no big difference between one sex or the other except for the boyish comfort of being able to urinate anywhere. But when I reached adolescence things began to happen at a dizzying pace. My voice changed, my body grew hair, and I found that my penis had a life of its own. I longed for the discretion of the female body when no amount of fantasizing would get me in trouble. As a man, instead, even the Sunday ritual of going to church with my family became an ordeal. I liked going to church. I even served as an altar boy, but as soon as the hormones began to run amok within me, going to church became a trial by erection. There were pretty girls in church, girls whose smells and giggles produced electric currents that inevitably found their way into my rising member. With difficulty, putting my hand inside the front pocket of my trousers, I managed to bend the thing sideways. Pretending devotion, kneeling on the pew, I'd close my eyes and think of the terrors of hell: infinite pits with burning cauldrons where I'd be submerged, angels targeting their arrows through my naked body, horrendous tortures of pulled teeth or fingernails. After a while I would feel the softening effects of such imaginings and recover enough composure to stand next to my parents at the end of the service to exchange greetings with their friends and acquaintances.

But I did become very curious and excited with the idea of having sex as a man. I had vague memories of my time as a woman. Vague, I repeat. Sometimes I didn't know from which life my memories came. Lounging around windows, visions of landscapes, smells, all of those were mingled in my different incarnations. They could have belonged to my life as a woman or as a dog or a cat. My memories as a parrot were the most distinct because of the sensation of flight. I recalled the bird's-eye view of large, green fields and the high-pitched sounds of the flock as we flew at sunset. I did remember sex as a woman, though. It was a memory of rustling skirts, being pitched against a wall, the pain, and a rod inching into me. Rough. It was the kissing I liked and that something which came up between my legs mingled with the pain, a tickling in my womb, indescribable. It had felt like submission nevertheless. Like being had, not having.

As a man, I gathered I would have, not be had. That seemed appealing to me, as did the anticipation of the physical feeling. I remembered that as a woman, I had put my fingers inside my vagina more than once. I had wondered what about it drove men crazy. I wanted to find out. It was my chance.

I had not envisioned the amount of work it would take. Girls were elusive and tricky. There was a disconnect between what they seemed to be willing to do and what they actually did. It was easy to be fooled. As a dog or a cat I could forgo the courtship. Not so as a man. Courtship seemed crucial. The right words, the right timing, even the first touch could make it or break it. What made it doubly difficult was looking at them: their skins, the way the roundness of their breasts emerged from their tank tops or the lacy, provocative things they wore, or to look at their rounded behinds inside their jeans and imagine peeling them like fruits. I had a thing for smells. Must have been from my life as a dog. It was so natural then to smell without any modesty, go straight for the cunts, the ass. Glorious. But I couldn't do that as a man, much as I wished I could. I had to make conversation, which was all right. Sometimes it was almost like smelling. Some girls could really dance with their words, create intricate tapestries in one's mind. But they were usually the most unreachable and time consuming. But it happened. Yes, it did. After I became proficient in the art of dating and courting, I scored. She was magnificent. Not a girl but a woman. A waitress. Gina. Dark and curvy and with a silky, deep voice. I didn't have to wine and dine her as much as others. We did drink a bottle of white wine. Then we walked to her place. We began to kiss. A woman's mouth is a thing in itself: the small teeth, the pointy tongue, and the breath, the sighs, the moaning when it starts to increase. It was then that I totally connected with my penis. It felt so right to have it advance, come forward, get ready like a swimmer aiming at the blue swimming pool, ready to launch into the deep, dreading and welcoming the experience at the same time. Would I make it? I thought. It was scary having such a voluptuous creature ready to go for it and not be sure one could deliver. Why not? I asked myself. At that moment every one of my past lives helped me. Having been a woman, I knew this was not about performance, but about being there, enjoying every minute, acknowledging the presence of another. She didn't need me to pleasure her. Besides I wanted to be inside of her so much. I really did. That was an experience I had not had. As a dog, cat, or parrot it's so different. No pleasure involved, but smells and mechanics, and a blinding instinct. Being a man, instead, inside of her, I felt the grab of the skin enveloping me, pulsing over me, soft and dense and powerful. I felt the force of the womb holding me, beckoning me deeper and deeper, and I felt her arms, her nails on my shoulders, her sounds exploding around me, and as I was coming, as the earth sang around me, I swore to live a good life, to be honorable and worthy, to do whatever was needed to become a true man and never again come back as a cat, a dog, or a parrot. As a woman, sure. After being inside a man's mind, I knew, it's just as good. Just as good.

Nicaraguan writer and activist Gioconda Belli is the author of *The Country Under My Skin* and *Infinity in the Palm of Her Hand.*

John Berger

W hen he was a kid—around four to six years old—he had a strong sense of Nature. Like most or all kids do. Often later this sense is dismantled and taken to pieces by Reason, competitiveness and other adult priorities.

Nature for him had the shape of an egg which surrounded him and everything that happened to him. More than that, it contained everything that existed. He pictured it as an egg because it was a container without corners. Outside it there was nothing. Nothing.

Most of what was inside it was invisible and nameless but very present, as present as his own two feet or the teeth in his mouth.

What he could observe of Nature and was visible was also inside the egg. An avenue of trees. A horse. A carrot. The moon. A hedgehog. A river. Each of these visible things had behind it countless invisible and nameless things to which it was related.

The visible thing was the messenger or sign of all the invisible things crowding and bustling behind it. The parentage between the visible and the invisible was, however, physical not symbolic.

For example, carrot was the messenger or envoy of redness, pointedness, root, sand, badger, filigree leaves, rain, a taste that goes to the roof of the mouth, penetration.

For the boy the uniqueness and the eloquence of a carrot depended on all these overlappings and connections which he could sense (with all his five senses) but could not identify or name.

And the boy told himself that when he became a man (he told himself this when he was alone)—when he became a man, he must never lose the egg.

————————————

JOHN BERGER, an English art critic, painter, and author, was born in 1926. He is the author of *A Painter of Our Time, G.*, which won the 1972 Booker Prize, and the essay collection *Ways of Seeing*.

Amy Bloom

Vera Williams hated the time between sets at the Nite Cap. The whole time was spent sweating and setting and refinishing her skin. Vitiligo never took a night off. Vera drank one big glass of water and one hot tea with honey in the nasty dressing room and she sat at the bar for only two minutes before she went back on. She did notice that when she made herself up as white, she was more conservative, all over. Light pink lipstick, pearl earrings, a tisket, a tasket. She didn't get as many chances, lately. Since the war started, people looked at each other a little more carefully. Negro and white people looked twice at dark-skinned white people, at Chinese and Japanese people, at people with accents. Before, if you said you were white, by God, people took you for white and if you said you were Negro, people certainly took you for Negro. Vera thought that it might be pushing her luck to impersonate a white woman too often, although she had an itch, every now and then, to bust out her Doris Day and she had the tight pink sheath and white gloves to do it. In Reno, she'd done Doris Day for about a week, with a white quartet behind her. The trumpeter wasn't really a man. He was a tubby, sweet-faced little guy and no one mentioned to his wife or three sons— and Vera had wondered about those three strapping boys—that he was really a tubby, sweet-faced gal who could swing all night on the trumpet and had decided that her chances were better if she wasn't a woman. Sometimes, in spite or annoyance, when the band stayed half a beat behind her all night, Vera'd imagine swiping a lipstick across the trumpeter's round face or pulling his pompadour forward into a pixie cut. It would only take one gesture and she would never be he again.

Sometimes, when Vera filled in her color, connecting all the blank seas and inlets to the smaller and smaller brown islands, it was hard not to feel that she was impersonating a Negro. The dark, arched eyebrows. Cherries in the Snow's ruby red cream filling in her pale, streaky upper lip. Her nose, which was sometimes a contouring challenge when she was white, was a comfort. It was a Negro nose. When she was Negro, she sometimes put a little beige cream down the bridge to broaden it, in case someone failed to notice. Once you slide around between the races, it becomes clear that most of race is an illusion. Political and necessary and historical but really, largely a matter of appearance. Like Rudolph Valentino's nose. How did people not notice that schnozz everywhere? You saw it on fancy white men from Philly to Boston. You saw it on half the Italians in New York, every other Tony and Guido. You saw it on almost every handsome colored flying ace, in newsreel after newsreel during the war. That bony arch and hawklike tip. How did people not see that it was the same nose? It was probably the same dick, too. Vera knew a girl who met Errol Flynn in Hollywood and she said it was no longer than your forefinger but as wide around as a biscuit and Vera heard the same was true of many Italian men and of the Tuskegee Fliers, too.

18 June 1943

Dear Miss Williams,

I am writing to you after an evening at the Nite Cap. I am the chap who bought you a stinger between sets, but you have so many admirers that that description may not help my cause. Your performance tonight was splendid. I think that Lena Horne herself would have applauded your "Stormy Weather" and your version of "Sentimental Journey" was truly beautiful. I will be at the Nite Cap next Sunday. If I may, I will again buy you a drink between sets.

Yours, in admiration,
Edward V. Moore

He did not say, I am the white man who bought you a drink, because it was possible that there'd been other white men at other shows, although he hadn't seen any. He felt that the letter had a little more Jeeves-and-the-country-house than he'd intended. He'd never used the word *chap* in his life, but he was an English butler in a Negro nightclub and it might be that his trump card was foolishness. Life as an English butler was not at all like the life he'd had as an English teacher, but the food was better, the pay was better, and the colleagues were, in the end, absolutely no worse.

Edward hadn't thought about how it would be inside the Nite Cap. He had a free Saturday night, which he rarely did. (Saturday night, the Torelli family usually had twenty or thirty relatives over for dinner and Edward tended bar, served the priests, supervised the buffet, and drove the resentful cousins he had not been able to keep out of Joe Torelli's Scotch back to the Bronx. "From whence they come," Joe Torelli said.) The Irish bars of Great Neck were rough and charmless and Manhattan was too big a pond. He wanted a place he could listen to jazz, where no one knew him and no one wanted to. He thought he wanted anonymity. And people in bars often do want to be nameless but they don't want to be invisible. If you want to be invisible, you stay home. Inside the Nite Cap, Edward was not invisible. He shone, and not in a good way. Edward had never been the only white man in a room full of Negro people. The bouncer was Negro, the tall, creamy coat-check girl was Negro, the broad-shouldered, bald-headed bartender and all of the men and women around him were Negro. At Windsor College, he was often the only man in a room full of women and it never bothered him. To be the sole man was not unpleasant; sometimes it was charming. Nice women rarely turn on a man they know, and even if they do, they're women; their weapons are words. The Nite Cap was filled with tired women who worked hard for their living, and a few working girls and men with nicked, thick hands and cut faces; laborers, cooks, truck drivers, fighters. After ten minutes at a rickety table, a waiter brought Edward a gin. He let go of Edward's glass reluctantly, not opening his hand until Edward gave him five dollars and told him to keep it. The waiter moved a little more briskly, as if service could now be expected. Edward's first impulse was appeasement. If he knew what would make these men smile, and these women forgive him, he would offer it. He would soft-shoe across the small stage, make fun of his own accent and pallor, demonstrating his essential harmlessness, so he could stay in the Nite Cap, and not get hurt.

1 July 1943

Dear Miss Williams,

   It was a pleasure to see you again. I fear that I may have interrupted your conversation with your colleague, the drummer, and I apologize. I'm delighted that you remembered encountering me outside the Silver Star Diner. I certainly remembered you. Would you consider joining me for an evening in Manhattan this coming Wednesday evening? My daughter is performing in an off-Broadway

show and I hoped we might watch her performance and have a late
supper at Gino's afterwards. I understand that Mr. Circiello is
quite a jazz fan and I'm sure he would be honored to have you at
his restaurant.

Edward saw that there would be some difficulties in courting
Vera. He was almost twenty years older. He was white. He was
not rich. (He wasn't certain that even by the standards of a Negro
jazz singer on Long Island, he qualified as good enough.) He gave
a lot of thought to which places would be welcoming to them as a
couple and he felt that Greenwich Village was his first choice. From
what he'd heard from Earl, the bartender at the Nite Cap, there
were a few nightclubs in Harlem that would be a distant second.

Vera, having been born and raised in America, didn't give it
a second thought.

"You do have your own home?" she said.

Edward and Vera walked down Hudson Street. It was a cool
night and Vera felt the wind right through her stockings. She was
sorry she hadn't worn her wool coat. Edward noticed. He said,
You'll meet my daughter another time, we must get you inside.
Vera thought that a man who put her comfort over his daughter's
pleasure and over his own plan was a man to see again and
Edward thought, Thank you for that, God. Dinner at Gino's was
what they both expected and they both liked Italian-American
food, for the way it was not what they were raised on. The food
covered the plate, the tomato sauce was mildly spicy and thick
and one could imagine a warmhearted chubby woman, who was
not like Edward's mother or Vera's, stirring a pot in the kitchen,
humming some Neapolitan tune. Mr. Circiello didn't welcome
them with any special attention but he didn't raise an eyebrow and
he gave them a good table and he did say "Good night, signorina,

good night, signor" and for Vera and Edward, the evening was a tremendous success. They had been seen and served and thanked. Edward drove them back to the house Vera shared, to the room she rented from a cousin of the drummer. They sat in the car. Edward put the radio on.

"Like a couple of kids," Vera said.

"You, of course, are a spring flower," Edward said. "I should be bringing you to the Ritz."

Vera sat still.

"You think if the Ritz was handy, you'd be taking me there?"

They were somewhere between banter and the bitterness of a woman who sees that the man doesn't know her worth. Edward's sympathies were entirely with Vera.

"Vera, I'm too old for you and I'm not rich. I want to take you out every evening that we are both free and I want us to go to the best clubs and eat dinner at places like Gino's, which I can hardly afford on a butler's salary. If I follow my impulses in this matter, I will have to steal the Torelli silver, pawn it at that place we passed tonight, and, unless I am very clever, spend the rest of my quiet life in the state penitentiary. Breaking rocks."

"I see that," Vera said. "I see you on the chain gang. I see you singing 'Diamond Joe' from can to can't."

"I do know 'Diamond Joe,'" Edward said.

"You do not."

"I may struggle with the tune," he said, and he sang, not badly and in no accent but his own.

Ain't gonna work in the country
And neither on Forester's farm
I'm gonna stay till my Marybelle come . . .
Will I stand this rotten old jail
Till the day I die?

Vera smiled and shook her head. Edward said, "Oh, I know. I cannot impress you." He leaned forward and kissed Vera on her neck and her cheek. He wanted to lick off her makeup, to kiss the perfect, variegated Vera underneath. She thought that it would be good if he did, it would be cool water on her blistered heart, if he did.

Amy Bloom is the author of five novels and short story collections, including *Where the God of Love Hangs Out*. She is currently working on her next novel, *Lucky Us*.

Darrell Bourque

I*t was raining on the Fontenots in Ville Platte and Mamou.*

I put on the wire-mesh mask my aunt made me first thing this morning. I didn't want to see myself in the usual way. Uncommon February thunder awakened me even earlier than I had expected and here I was in the fading dark with my brother. He was adjusting the padding in the brassiere my grandmother had given him to wear. He was going as her as a young girl, big tits, big ass already even as a young girl. She had also given him a pair of her old drawers and advice on how to pad them too, and an evening dress of hers she had kept for years in her old hope chest.

. . . raining on the Meauxs and Soileaus in Iota and Kaplan.

I was going to run in the traditional costume: capuchon reminiscent of medieval days and my loosely fitting smock and pajama-like pants, a hospital green scrub suit my uncle wore on rounds. My great-grandmother gave me rectangles of brightly colored rags from her basket of quilting material to sew onto that green background so that when I ran with the other boys to catch chickens for the gumbo we would make that night, I would be a flurry of sorts, the sewn-on tags working me like tesserae in mosaics.

. . . raining on the Daigles and Thibodeauxs in Church Point.

I didn't want to see Joe or T-boy, or Beau, or So-Lay or any of those other names I answered to. Today I didn't want to be Joseph Clarence Beausoleil Broussard, my name after my grandfather whose clarity was always somewhat obscured by his love of the bottle and Beausoleil after my oldest ancestor with his sunny smiling face itself a mask for his guerrilla life. I didn't not want to not be like them exactly but I wanted to be something else too, even if just for today on this day of fools.

    … raining on the Cheramis and Voisins in Chauvin and Cocodrie.

We would join the older men in a few hours. We would ride horses through the countryside. We would be followed by wagons filled with fiddlers and accordion players, boys with triangles and frottoirs. Like malfacteurs from some ancient time, we would fill the air with sound and we would dismount at every house begging for money or chickens or anything we could get, and we would dance in mud or dust or whatever the ground was like on any given day. Today it would be mud for sure.

    … raining on the Oliviers and Sigues and Bouttes in Grand Marais.

From the start we'd take our brothers in our arms, sing and dance, chase chickens through fields and pastures, jump ditches, crawl under houses if we had to. We'd get caught up in the act. We'd be fire and air. We'd be for those who watched us from the sidelines those fools and cross-dressers and grotesques caught in a suffering we could not dance away. We'd be the remnant of a dream they are about to be absorbed into.

    … raining on the Delafosses and Thierrys and Guillorys in Mallet.

I knew as I looked at myself through the wire in this half light that something had gone wrong somewhere or just had not been discovered yet about who and what we were. I knew on this day when everything could go every-which-way that there was a truth in the every-which-way. On the day of fools the march of history made no sense. If everything went in one direction only, it was just not true, today or on any other day. I never for one day felt like an *idée reçue,* and I knew received ideas were lies, taints.

...raining on the Ancelets and Guilbeaus and Babineauxs in Beau-bassin.

Tonight, back at the starting point, those who watched and laughed at us will make a meal. Some of us will change into cleaner, drier clothes. We will eat and drink together, at least until midnight. We will dance again and again, at least until midnight. Then we will all go home. Underneath the madness and costuming are mostly lonely boys grieving the untold ways they are shortchanged by desire. When I take my clothes off at the end of the day, I don't want to not be like everyone of them. But when I take the wire-mesh mask off, I want to look at myself and see Joe again, and Beau and So-Lay and T-Boy. I want to see that old proverbial fool too, my drunk grandfather perhaps, stepping with torn pants into the abyss as a new idea, and I want to follow him wherever he is going.

———

DARRELL BOURQUE is the author of six collections of poetry. He is a professor emeritus at the University of Louisiana at Lafayette and former poet laureate of Louisiana.

John Boyne

There he is now, standing on the bridge over the DART line at Blackrock Station, all nine years and four and a half feet of him. He's short for his age and skinny with it. His brothers are tall lads, every one. The oldest props his teacup on the boy's head as a joke whenever he has a girl over. So he's short, but he's big enough to put one foot in the gap between the iron bars and hoist himself up so he's sitting on top, legs dangling, looking out across the Irish Sea towards a fog-hidden Howth Head.

He has five of them—brothers, that is—and a father. No mother. She died nine years ago. He came into the world, she went out of it. His father is house-proud. Vacuums, cleans, polishes. Lifts things up, rubs a cloth underneath. Shoes off at the front door. They don't live far from here, just down the road on Seapoint Avenue.

"You're a lucky boy," Mr. Next-Door tells him. "I was the only lad in a houseful of women. I had seven sisters and a mammy. Daddy died when his milk float met a Rolls-Royce on Gardiner Street." Mr. Next-Door seems proud of this; his chest puffs visibly when he says the words *Rolls-Royce*. His bare chest. The chest that he likes the boy to kiss when he's teaching him. Daddy taught him, he tells the boy, before the collision on Gardiner Street. He's passing the lessons along. Every boy should learn how to be a man.

There's a bit of rain falling, nothing too heavy, but he turns his face up towards the sky and closes his eyes, letting it fall on him, wash him clean. Mr. Next-Door likes to give him a bath after his lessons. "This would be your mammy's job," he tells him, "if she was still with us." He rubs the flannel across the boy's abdomen. "Your mother was a lovely woman," he says. "A saint. It's a shame you never knew her."

He remembers the day his geography teacher took the class on a boat across to Howth Head for the morning. They were going to look at the flora and fauna, he said. The boys were to write down everything they saw and Danny Masters, who was tops at art, was to do a few drawings for the classroom wall. He talked to them about Howth as if it were a foreign country. They didn't see much in the end. A few rock pools with frogs, slime, and an old discarded boot lying in the centre. Danny Masters drew a picture of the geography teacher taking a pee behind a bush. There was war over it.

A quick wind nearly unseats him and he grips the girder. Looking down he can see the train tracks and thousands of little stones between the lines. This way to Dun Laoghaire, to Dalkey, to Greystones; that way to Lansdowne Road, to Connolly, to Malahide. There are no mice. One of his brothers likes to tell the story of the time he was in the London underground and he counted forty-two mice running between the tracks while he waited on the Jubilee line for a train out to Bermondsey where the mother of a girl he liked was insisting on having him over for his tea. The things we do for a ride, he told the boy, who thought he was talking about the journey.

A train must be due for the platform is starting to populate. Two old women, wrapped up in coats, gloves, and headscarves, their purses on strings tied to the inner lining. A boy reading a paperback book with a picture of mountains on the front. A girl listening to music. She looks up and sees him sitting there; doesn't react in any way. Her fingers scroll through, she chooses a different song.

He can see the train coming now from Booterstown and feels a sense of calm at what he has to do. He looks down at the platform again, at a man in an overcoat and hat, reading his ticket intently as if it's a new Harry Potter. It's Mr. Next-Door. He's biting the nails of his left hand, those same fingers that he uses to play with the boy. The train chugs towards the station; the wind picks up. He takes his hands off the bridge, feels his body unsettle, stretches his arms out like he's ready to take flight as a woman below lets out a scream, the train screeches its horn and he leans forward to let himself go. This is how, he thinks as he falls. This is how. This is how to fly.

———

Irish writer JOHN BOYNE is the author of *The Boy in the Striped Pajamas,* which was made into a film by the same name. His latest novel is *This House Is Haunted.*

James Lee Burke

My father lost his best friend on the last day of the Great War. As a consequence, he despised all wars and the men who created them and who lived vicariously through the suffering they caused. I learned from my father that there is an inherent danger in mass movements of any kind. The temptation is to join in lockstep with others, under a common banner, and give oneself over to emotional demands that are always presented to us as a means of achieving a greater good, at the expense of conscience and self-respect.

It takes courage to say no to martial rhetoric and the authority of ignorance. It takes courage to be gentle and kind. It's no fun to be ostracized. But is there anything worse than being a member of the herd, a sycophant who serves the perverse abstractions that others have created for him? And isn't there a wonderful sense of victory in one's chest if one can swallow his blood and let the world break its fist on his face and never show his pain?

More simply put, when a man can grin and walk through the cannon smoke and give no heed to those who hurt him, he drives the bad guys up the wall.

A man makes his troth with his own vision of this world and perhaps the unseen one that lies just beyond it, and he stays true to his principles and doesn't keep score. Toward the top of the ninth inning, the math on the scoreboard over the center field fence usually looks pretty good.

———

JAMES LEE BURKE was born in Houston, Texas, in 1936. He's won two Edgar Awards and is the author of over twenty books, including *Light of the World: A Dave Robicheaux Novel*.

Gabriel Byrne

In the shop window, Khrushchev and Kennedy flickered, white and black, on a seventeen-inch Pye television screen. (It was yours for ten shillings and six pence per week on the never-never, missus.)

It was an electrical shop and a gentlemen's outfitters, Carneys, all windows, no walls. The leaders of the world sat right there, voiceless to me, behind the glass, among sports coats and hoovers and transistor radios. And Ned the postman who read lips on account of his eldest being deaf shuffled up beside me, smelling of Woodbine. The rain came down, no surprise. Ned narrated to me a fearful language never heard before. Death and hell. Rivers on fire. Hills of molten lava snaking along the streets. We will bury you. The flesh was falling from the bones of those I loved, and all the mountain flowers were crushed and broken.

All the next day the rain kept falling, falling. And out over the fields my grandfather and I tramped to bring home, in their sodden innocence, the beasts of the field for milking. The dark angels screeched for worms in the new-turned earth and I— yesterday a boy, made man now by knowledge that presently all must end forever—stood beneath the dripdropping branches while my grandfather drew the smoke of his cigarette deep down into himself and let it out. And for a moment the smoke was one with the breath of cattle.

And in that moment, young and old were speaking in an ancient silence, understanding nothing, everything, and all the world was made eternal.

———

Irish actor GABRIEL BYRNE has starred in more than forty films, including *Miller's Crossing* and *The Usual Suspects*. He won a Golden Globe for his performance on *In Treatment*.

Aifric Campbell

It's 4:08 when my brother comes strolling onto the trading floor. The ticker tape glides sweetly overhead, the markets are all wrapped up, and I'm basking in the screen glow of a rich, lazy peace. Outside, the city is doused in Thanksgiving cheer.

"You still carry that round?"

Al looks down like he's forgotten the little blue book in his hand.

"Chuck it here."

I run my finger over the gold lettering.

BARRON'S
Dictionary of Finance and Investment Terms
Over 2,500 terms clearly defined and explained

Covers stocks, bonds, banking corporate finance and more

"Remember the day he gave it to us?"

"Take Our Sons to Work Day. Fifth grade."

"The Federal Reserve."

Al puffs his chest into Dad mode. *Check it out, boys. Only one way in and one way out.*

"The Gold Vault."

"Fifty feet below sea level."

"Five hundred and thirty thousand gold bars."

"You fell in love."

It's true—I was dizzy, almost faint, swooning beneath the glittering wall. *For thine is the kingdom.* Dad stood like a plinth between us. *You boys wanna piece of that?* I could only nod. The insides of my stomach were blowtorched by a new hunger: to have and to hold.

How about you, Al, you wanna piece of that?

I'm thinking about Midas, Al murmured, hand raised like he was shielding his eyes from the glare. *How everything he touched turned to gold.*

We should all have that gift, Dad laughed, ruffled Al's hair, and winked at the tour guide.

And then Midas hugged his daughter and she turned into a statue.

That night I scaled a golden cliff in a dream. Al crashed out of his bed at 3:00 A.M. and woke the house screaming he was Tutankhamen buried alive in a federal tomb. *Fucking Egyptians,* Dad scowled over his OJ at the cut in Al's brow.

"Remember how you memorized the whole thing, Al?" I flick through the stubby Barron's, the worn pages curiously untearable. It was the words he loved: "alligator spread—alien corporation—aged fail—air pocket," he'd chant them by torchlight, like the secret language was the real treasure. He learnt the definitions by heart. I learnt the business and got ahead.

"Ever think of all the words that *aren't* in Barron's?" he says, but it's an Al question, he's not listening for an answer, he's just thinking aloud and watching the tape. Though he doesn't see what I see: the price of everything laid out before us, the whole world neatly named and tagged. Al's always finding value that no one else can fathom.

Like that feral half-breed at summer camp he tried to tame who bit his hand. Those skinny vegans he brought home, girls with legs like deer who liked poetry but had no respect for real things.

"Here." I toss back the book.

"Read it. Learn it. Then go out and fucking do it."

"All set for the early start tomorrow?"

"Can't wait. The Happy Thanksgiving."

"You know, Al, you could just shut the fuck up sometimes. Not take his bait."

"Quit worrying about me." He gives me the big blue-eyed grin. "I don't."

"Bull and Bear? Me and the guys had a big day here."

"You always ask."

"And you always say no."

We were backslapped on to the same track, except mine is fast now and Al's is slow and slowing, like a carriage uncoupled. Soon my little brother will be a stick man on the career horizon. *Eleven months and two weeks. That's how long it takes for genetic code to unravel.* But there he goes now, tall and straight-backed, cruising unruffled through the double doors.

"In here, boys," Dad calls from the kitchen, where the beached bird lies on its back in a big platter. The oven trembles, waiting. Heat shimmers like a mirage in the sunslashed window. The dog's tail swishes the stone floor. Somewhere upstairs is the sound of Mom hovering.

Dad plonks his Bud on the counter, rolls up his sleeves.

"Think of this turkey as your client." He clasps the goose-bumped bird between both palms, tenderly, like he's trying not to startle it.

"First you gotta get to know him." His right hand caresses the naked breast, his left slips soft and slow over the thighs. "Then you gotta care for him." He strokes the plump curves.

Reaches for the pack of turkey frills and slides a little white boo-
tie onto each foot.

"That's better," he nods, and gently splays the legs. "You gotta
look after your client like your girl."

His fist slams into her asshole. He twists deep, hard. Grunts.
Withdraws.

He picks up the bottle and slugs. Slaps his free arm on my
shoulders, but he's not watching me, he's watching Al, whose eyes
are trained on the window and a view of the wide blue sky.

"We are the hollow men." Al lays both hands on the troubled
bird. "We are the stuffed men."

Dad snorts a beer guffaw. The spray catches Al's hands but he
doesn't look down.

"One of your fag English poets?"

"American, in fact." Al turns to face him, his gold hair shiny
now in the streaming sun. "The banker poet."

He steps in close, places a hand on our father's chest, like he's
checking for heartbeat. "This is the dead land."

Dad's mouth flips open. I hold my breath. But he's got nothing.

Irish writer AIFRIC CAMPBELL is the author of *The Se-
mantics of Murder*, as well as *On the Floor*. She formerly
worked at Morgan Stanley, where she was the first female managing director of the London trading floor.

Ron Carlson

When you move left for a hard-hit ground ball and misplay it and it goes between your legs and on into left field allowing the runner on third to score the winning run, don't look in your mitt as if the ground ball which would have saved the day is in there because it is not. Stand up straight and remove your glove and carry it by the thumb in your off hand. Walk with your chin at altitude toward the dugout. Keep your eyes open. Do not grimace. Look for the coach's face and when you find it, look him in the eye and nod. You know what happened.

RON CARLSON is the director of the MFA program in fiction at the University of California–Irvine, and the author of ten books. His latest novel is *Return to Oakpine*.

Bill Cheng

I

By dawn, you could already smell it—ice and dust. I went up to the canopy and sure enough, there it was: large and blue and looming, a massive tooth overlooking the valley. I watched it groan, breaching into the grasslands. The endless winter. The end of the world.

That night, I thought about my old pa—that miserable bullying son of a bitch, thumping his breast and flashing those fangs.

"Things I seen, boy. Make your mane go white."

And he'd turn back those oily eyes and touch the smoothness below his spine.

"You'll get yours too, won't you?" he'd said. "Your test. Your try."

So I leaned in against the dark, my soul rumbling, while the females picked the nits from off my coat.

II

And in the plainlands, the grass went silver and the trees flashed to crystal. We watched from our forest, huddled and tense. The lashing wind. The snow in everything and everywhere, we thought the land would choke.

III

We strapped our young'uns to our backs and I led our people down to the forest floor. I listened—the crash of leaves. Our silent weight against the bark. Descending from bough to bough, the ground rising beneath us. Everything we had, everything we were, was up in the trees and leaving—it was like climbing down our own throats.

That night we slept in the brush and we ate ants and millipedes—and we hated the world. For days, I had the runs and it was impossible to sleep. Not with the wrenching in your gut and tigers in the brambles.

IV

We died like flies. Starved or murdered or hunted for our meat. One day we found something in the weeds. It was limp and rubbery and fatting maggots. We gathered around, snuffling and shivering. It'd been almost all the time now but this one wasn't more than a few weeks old. The dark mat of fur. Its small red fingers like berries.

It was one of ours, not long dead.

Talk started about turning back, returning to the trees. An argument broke and there were heated words about wanting to break off, splinter into a rival tribe. Wasn't long before things turned ugly—all teeth and claws and brother's blood. They drummed their chests and bared their fangs and beat each other's asses into the dust.

There wasn't time—not for this.

So I drew up my breath and smoothed my feet against the earth. I eased the weight from off the knuckles, and as I reared and stood—two feet anchored—my shadow like a great hand reaching—they quieted and turned and saw what I was—what they could be, and they knew we would not go back into the trees.

V

From that day on we were unstoppable. We ravaged the land, raining hellfire and damnation upon the valley. What I wanted, I took—and the rival tribes were laid to waste. We were like gods, tearing through the western territories, stealing their females and slaughtering every knuckle-dragging son of a bitch we saw.

VI

The first I ever killed was a rival chief. A big son of a bitch with a gorgeous fiery coat. He was twice my size but I wrestled him down, and I caved his head with a rock. I remember afterwards I went down to the stream and I couldn't stop shaking. My arms ached. My head buzzed. I waded out into the deep, his tooth still in my neck. It stung when it touched the water. And when I climbed out—the murder-rock still in my bleeding hand—I felt the last of my fur slipping off the skin.

VII

That was some time ago now, before the snow and the ice and the howling winds; before the caves; before the endless winter. But I remember standing above the grasses. The whole damn valley lay there and I saw the beasts of the wild, where sky meets the fields, the sun over everything.

Sometimes I dream about the old days. The high sweet air. The boughs flexing against my weight. The wind that parts the trees.

And now the snow is piling up, dull and cottony, and I feel old as hell.

I look at our tribe, the new blood, still hungry and frightened and murder-minded. Sometimes, when the hunting parties are away, I'll dip my hand into the char and press my palm to the wall. Then I will step away and sometimes I think I see it. Out among the buffalo and wild horses—some hint. Some clue of what we should be. Or I'll look outside and there're days I don't think the snow will ever end. And sometimes, I think—well goddamn, won't it have to?

BILL CHENG was born in Queens and lives in Brooklyn. His debut novel, *Southern Cross the Dog,* was published in May.

Scott Cheshire

I was in a loincloth, pale parts on display, face pressed into a white plastic doughnut. The view all carpet. Still afraid of needles, so the focus helped, but acupuncture is mostly waiting so I waited for the very first sting. When? Where? My forehead? Carotid? How deep? And will I bleed? I saw the glossy brochures fanned on the waiting-room table, and it looked like a freak show to me. Ladies and Gentlemen: The Human Pincushion.

Trophy of my youth, Paula, the good wife, she made the appointment.

She knew I didn't like doctors—hospitals, dentists, I don't care. I don't like charts of my insides up on a wall like calendar pages. And she knew about the needles. A little bit. It's not something you hide easy. I'd fainted at our pre-wedding blood test.

She said, He's not that kind of doctor.

It wasn't the pain. I know pain. In fact, redheads need more anesthetic. The ginger feels too much, and no matter how much a dentist numbs my gums, I feel it.

She said, It could help with your temper.

Temper? You're the one with a temper, I said, so throw your accusations out the window.

She said, And maybe it'll help with your downstairs business.

Downstairs business? If you want to talk downstairs, this was practically opposite. New Agey disco breathing out from the walls.

A heat lamp toasting my backside. Exposed. And the man—at first I refused to call him a doctor—he bikinied my loincloth, folding it over my glutes, a between-thigh tuck. His hands were fearless. The man actually got on *top* of me, cracking my back, not to mention the left shoulder—a trouble spot, from college, rugby, an unexpected victory-dance kerfuffle, so I wondered how did he know? I felt his warm hand there against my shoulder, kneading harder, deeper. Was this it? The first needle? Finally? Now?

Then like a prick at my finger, I felt it.

Not so bad...

But then he pressed the needle even deeper, deep in the muscle of my shoulder. A low electrical charge. My shoulder pulsing, a tickle of wires falling at my back, I imagined a toy set of jumper cables.... The muscle pulsing like the beating of my heart. I fell into a reverie, a deep and near-sleeping dream....

Lovely wife. What happened to us? Trying for two years, I'd hardly delivered. Was it physical? Mental? I knew this—fathers are a complicated business. Also that I'd been spending too many nights at the neighborhood bar, alone, and sipping High Lifes. The sort of place my father loved, grumbling with the other ex-husbands. We hadn't spoken in years, and still I protected the man. The day before the needles, Paula said: You're not like him, you never will be. The man has no balls.

She could have said: The same goes for you, Mr. Small-Minded. Step it up, and let's have a family.

But she didn't. Because she mercifully loves me.

What did I say? You wanna talk about fathers? To the bone—I said things I swore I'd never say out loud.

Forgive me!

The muscle matching my heart, it was pulsing...

Don't move, he said, pulling needles from my Achilles, the cabling from my shoulder. He patted my back, sit straight.

I sat there awash in beige, light-headed, hazily aware of what happened. I'd lost time. But the shoulder was feeling better. I was at peace, a vague stirring in my loins....

I said, I feel good. Tell me how?

He took my hand. His white pants and shirt, crisp, Mr. Clean. He said, It's sort of like fly-fishing.

Fly-fishing? What did he know about fly-fishing? Manhandling grown men, dressed up like an ice-cream salesman.

Here, he said, and tapped a needle into the web of my thumb. Just above the nerve.

Then again, what did I know of fly-fishing?

Cast for the nerve, he said. But don't catch it. It's way too painful. Catch the Qi, right above it. Energy. Life.

Qi? Energy? I didn't speak his language. I was hazy, coming around, and dumbfounded.

He touched my shoulder. How do you feel?

How did he know? I nodded....

He turned to leave.

I said: Wait.

Would a handshake suffice? The man had really touched me. I said, I need to call the wife.

Okay.

Another stirring, I wanted to cover my lap. And when was the last time I really wanted my wife? I was thrilled by the thought, and starved, ravenous. Dazed. Where was my phone? What did I owe? A feeling I couldn't explain, it was electric. A sudden compulsion to hug the man, I steeled myself. I said, Doctor.

I extended my hand.

SCOTT CHESHIRE's forthcoming debut novel, *High as the Horses' Bridles,* will be published by Henry Holt.

Ed Conlon

There was something satisfying in the numbers, at least, when Kiko was killed. He was shot six times, as he stood with five other men, at four in the morning. Three men in a car—two shooters and a driver—hit two victims, one fatally. The survivor was Kiko's nephew Gordo, and he had as little to say as the dead man. Less, if you counted what Kiko had tattooed in slant capitals across the yard of back fat between his shoulder blades: kill all rats. Kiko was a drug dealer who had spent more than a decade in prison. Kiko wasn't a rat. Even the bullet holes that riddled his torso looked like little angry mouths, shut tight. So the final number was zero, for arrests, which wasn't very satisfying at all. This was years ago, in the Bronx. It was my case.

The possibilities weren't infinite, but they seemed vast, at first. All of Kiko's friends were felons, too. They were from different parts of the city, with their own histories of grudges and feuds; the night before, they had been at five or six bars, bumping into hundreds of other revelers. Despite their pasts, the felons were decent enough guys, seemingly sincere in their desire to help. I couldn't fault them for failing to identify faces, under fire, from across a dark street after eight hours of Heinekens and Hennessy. Gordo, the nephew, didn't have much of a record, but he was useless on principle, denying that he recognized any mug shots even before I opened the folder. I'd found out who had done it, soon enough.

Years before, Kiko had run into a man named Javonne in one of the same bars, and he'd sliced his throat with a box cutter. Javonne was a drug dealer, too, but the beef was over a girl, probably, but maybe over a dirty look, or a spilled drink. It was over nothing. Javonne barely made it to the hospital, but he refused to talk, even after his severed vocal cords were reattached. Knowing what had happened made the lack of proof all the more painful. I thought I had the second shooter, too, when he was also shot, the day after Kiko was killed, and Javonne drove him to the hospital. That turned out to be unrelated. As far as finding anyone who was willing to step up and speak out, I was in no-man's-land. I could have been out in the desert wastes, or adrift on the arctic ice.

I'd come across Raquel from a cell phone subpoena, weeks into the case, after all the other leads had gone nowhere. There had been dozens of conversations between her and Javonne, mostly late at night. I went to visit her at her house in the suburbs on a Sunday morning. Her husband answered the door. As the three of us sat around the kitchen table, I said that I'd been told that she knew a person named Javonne, who was involved in a crime in the Bronx. Raquel looked like an ant under a magnifying glass when her husband glared at her. She denied everything. I knew she was lying, but I didn't push very hard. I wasn't with the adultery police.

Detectives sometimes work the way the devil is supposed to, in whispered insinuations that wear you down like water on stones. Javonne was scared when I finally brought him in, and I talked to him all night about what Kiko had done to him. I told him about how many of his friends I knew, about what they'd done, what had been done to them. I talked about his children. I knew their names and ages. Once or twice, he came close to breaking, but he never did.

What I couldn't tell him was that I'd been in touch with the feds, and he was facing a drug rap that would put him away for longer than murder would in the Bronx. That message wasn't for me to deliver. But when I let him out, the next morning, I mentioned that I'd gone to see Raquel.

He smiled at first, and then the line of his mouth twisted, as if there were a fishhook in his lip. He scratched his eye, and rubbed his brow.

"Yeah, well. It's a shame with . . . what happened."

And then I could have been back in no-man's-land, lost in the icy waste, for all I had to say, for all I had to ask about Raquel. I hadn't done wrong, I knew. So I kept telling myself. Still, I heard whispers in my head for a long time after. A man has to know when to keep his mouth shut.

ED CONLON is a former NYPD officer and the author of *Blue Blood* and *Red on Red*.

Sloane Crosley

—————

You hear a lot of things growing up about how to be a man. Some of it is stuff you can control, like pulling chairs out for women or having an impressive life skill or manning up when some kid nails you in the nuts with a baseball. Then one day you realize that all the stuff you've been told is actually not *for* you. It's for what other people think of you. But you're alone so much, even when you're married. In the shower or falling asleep or in your own head. Alone. I mean, I'm writing this on the toilet. I've got the newspaper on the floor, my laptop on one knee and a salad bowl filled with Cap'n Crunch on the other knee. Manliness is about balance, friends. Balance.

—————

SLOANE CROSLEY, the author of the essay collections *I Was Told There'd Be Cake* and *How Did You Get This Number,* is at work on her first novel.

Michael Cunningham

Several years ago, I met a man named Buck Angel, who had been born a woman. Men who were born women are, of course, easy to meet by now.

Unlike most transgendered people, however, Buck elected to become a man, but retain his central girl-part.

We're accustomed to chicks with dicks. A guy with a pie is still something of a rarity.

Buck, who lives in San Francisco, was the featured performer at the Black Party, an annual all-night-and-into-the-morning event held in New York City at the vast and crepuscular Roseland Ballroom, which attracts uncountable hordes, almost all of them gay men.

It's "black" in that most men turn up in leather harnesses, chaps, chrome-studded armbands, and other S&M gear. Some are actual leather daddies (and the boys who love them). Some keep their leather stashed away, and bring it out once a year. A guy at the Black Party might appear to be fetish-y, but may spend most of his other 364 nights watching TV with his husband, after the kids are in bed. Nevertheless, on Black Party night, husbands and fathers manage to look every bit as tough and glowering as everybody else.

I'd heard of Buck Angel, in some vague way. I was curious. And so, was more than glad to learn that a friend of mine knew him slightly, and could arrange an introduction backstage, before Buck went out and danced naked for the multitudes.

I'm not entirely sure what I was expecting of Buck, but it had to do, in my imagination, with amorphousness, a neither-this-nor-that aspect. I suppose I'd pictured someone in a flesh-colored bodysuit that was, in Buck's case, his actual body.

Once my friend and I finagled our way backstage, I didn't think anything of it when a muscular, tattooed guy, wearing only a leather Speedo, ambled by. I assumed he was just another of the Black Party celebrants. In addition to their outfits, the men who come to the Black Party tend to have muscles and tattoos, to keep their hair buzzed, and maintain a perpetual three-day growth of stubble. There went another one.

My friend called out, "Hey, Buck, I've got somebody who wants to meet you."

Buck turned, smiled, offered a large and manly hand, bigger than mine (though I try not to focus overmuch on size questions). He said "Hey," in a cordial, dudely voice. I said "Hey" back.

There wasn't much for us to talk about, and Buck was due onstage in a couple of minutes. I like to think I can converse with pretty much anyone, but standing before Buck, I couldn't seem to come up with anything better than, "How do you like New York?"

Buck assured me that he did. I may have said something about the weather in San Francisco.

I was dumbstruck. Buck, the epitome of masculine camarade-rie, told me it had been good to meet me, that he hoped I was having a good time at the Black Party, and, hey, sorry man, I've got to go out there and earn my keep.

As I watched him depart, I had an unobstructed view of his muscular back, his narrow hips, and perfect man-ass.

Buck wasn't only an entirely convincing man. He was an en-tirely convincing gay man, of a certain type. Grapefruit-sized biceps, encircled by spiky tribal tattoos. Washboard abs. Hair as cropped as a soldier's, short enough for the scalp to shine pinkly through.

Buck, however, had once been a girl. A pretty little girl. (I Googled him afterwards, of course.) I hadn't imagined it was possible to so utterly transform not only one's body, but one's persona. Buck is a man. If you met him and didn't know his history, you'd entertain no doubts. Here's a handsome, awesomely fit, friendly, macho gay guy.

That night I went out into the audience, to see Buck in action. He emerged to cheers and whoops from the assembled masses. He grinned—he was not one of those detached, behold-my-godlike-perfection go-go dancers who tend to dominate the field. He started moving to the music, and whipped off the leather Speedo in one smooth move. (Velcro has revolutionized stripping.)

Yes. Between his legs there was, in fact, a vagina. No question.

We are, as a species, in love with self-invention. Walt Whitman, a schoolteacher and sometime journalist from Long Island, starts writing poetry in his mid-thirties, grows a beard, ties a bandanna around his neck, and wanders the streets of Manhattan, declaiming, "I sing the body electric." He becomes an icon.

Margarita Carmen Cansino, a Hispanic girl from Brooklyn, dyes her hair red and becomes Rita Hayworth. Scrawny, homely little Farrokh Bulsara, who's shown no particular gift for singing, leaves Zanzibar to go to art school in London, joins a ragtag local band for the hell of it, and becomes Freddie Mercury. Robert Zimmerman leaves the suburbs of Minnesota and arrives in New York as Bob Dylan, an amalgam of Woody Guthrie, James Dean, and young Robert's own ideas about himself as a tough, street-smart troubadour.

These aren't just impersonations. They're transformations.

These are people who *became* the figures they invented. There is no more Margarita Carmen Cansino, or Robert Zimmerman. There is no more Farrokh Bulsara. In old photographs, they look like their own ancestors.

That night at the Black Party, cheering Buck on among a crowd of men who'd been born men, and who looked more or less exactly *like* Buck, I realized that these biological males—the stubbled and muscled and tattooed—were in a variety of what I can only call flesh drag. Many of them had been sweet little boys. Many of them had been too sweet for their own good, and had been tortured by the bullies who thrive everywhere.

As they grew up, they turned themselves into somebody else. They changed not only their bodies, but their natures. They were more masculine than most straight men.

It would be silly not to wonder if they'd modeled their new, improved versions on the very same guys who once, years ago, played keep-away with their sack lunches, hid their French horns, and ducked their heads into boys' rooms toilets. Who can blame them for wanting to become somebody with whom bullies do not fuck around?

In the course of their transfigurations, though, they've become as imitate-able as Bette Davis or Judy Garland. Butch version. But still.

What, then, about the suburban dad, waiting in the Home Depot checkout line in polo shirt and Dockers? Is that what he really wants to wear? He probably doesn't think about his clothes much at all. But isn't there an element of impersonation? *If I look like a regular family man, I'll be a regular family man.*

RuPaul once said, "You're born naked, and everything after that is drag." I might add, Any outfit that's immediately identifiable is drag, by definition. There's not much of a market for go-go boys who gyratingly remove polo shirts and Dockers. But if a go-go boy came onstage in that particular outfit, you'd know who he was pretending to be.

Anyway.

There, that night, dancing to wild approbation, was the sine qua non of self-reinvention: the little girl who'd become a man. You could say, well, not quite, not entirely. But you could just as easily say, yes, entirely. You could say Buck insisted that manliness didn't depend on the possession, or acquisition, of a dick and a set of balls. You could say Buck stands as evidence that maleness, true maleness, isn't really about genitalia at all. It's a conviction. It's a costume that weds itself to your skin and, ultimately, penetrates your very being.

Men. I mean, what are we, anyway?

MICHAEL CUNNINGHAM is the author of *The Hours*, which won the PEN/Faulkner Award and the Pulitzer Prize, and most recently, *By Nightfall*.

Roddy Doyle

Becoming a man was easy enough in Ireland. The thing was easily learnt. You grew up hearing the words "How are you," all day. It looked like a question but it wasn't. It was never a question; that was the rule. Only nuts and the loners tried to make a question out of it, to snare you, to stop you from getting past them.

The responses were easily learnt too.

—Grand.

—Great.

—Not too bad.

—Okay—yeah.

—Alright.

And there was the new one that had arrived with the recession.

—I'm superb.

There was no getting past that one. A man could meet a man.

—How are yeh.

—I'm fuckin' superb.

And stay a man. No question had been asked and no answer was needed or wanted. Say nothing. That was how to be a man.

That was just stupid, of course. Pat knew that. But a chap from up the road had just told him he was superb when Pat was out in the front garden throwing a bag into the green wheelie and he couldn't avoid your man going past, heading off on his jog. Pat had wanted to lean over the wall and slap him.

Superb—for fuck sake. The jogger had a teenage daughter with cuts on her arms, a wife who was some sort of an Internet swinger, and a career that had been shot in the head a few months back. And the poor fucker wasn't built for jogging. He'd have been quicker rolling down the street. But, still, according to himself, he was superb. He was out of sight but Pat could hear him wheezing. Fucked, but still a man.

Pat went back inside. The house was empty. There was just himself. He didn't mind that. He was getting the hang of it. The boy was out somewhere, and that was good.

Women were no better. Although they probably talked more. "How are you?" was a question in the world of the women. They stopped and they answered. But the noise they made was no more honest than silence.

More shite—Pat knew. These generalizations about women and men. There was no depth to them, or truth. It was just—. He didn't know what it was. He'd never thought about it before, really. Men of few words, women of lots. That was his world. Always had been. He hated being in the company of men who talked too much and he'd fallen in love with the sound of his wife's voice, before he'd even seen her properly. And if that was sexist or something, he didn't care; he didn't give a fuck. He'd always done his fair share of the dishes, the clothes, the rearing. He'd never hidden money from her, or messed. So he could say what he fuckin' well wanted. He'd earned his opinions. He'd loved her.

He hated being angry.

He went to fill the kettle and found it was already full, and warm. He'd no memory of filling it, or turning it on. It didn't matter.

He didn't think the anger was right. It was like someone else invading him. It wasn't how he felt. How he wanted to feel. Sad, devastated. Stoical—was that the word?

But angry was how he felt. Furious.

He couldn't tell anyone.

He'd tried to break through it. He'd tried to talk to the boy, to get him to talk back. To let him know it was fine. He could say anything he wanted. Shout, cry. Anything that felt right.

—How are you? he'd asked—he'd asked.

—Grand, said the boy.

He'd left it at that, and tried again another day.

—How are you getting on?

—Yeah, grand, said the boy.—Okay—yeah.

—Good.

They weren't trained for it. They were men.

More shite.

A few weeks before the end he'd heard her on the phone. She was sitting at the window and she looked like she was melting in the sun. That fuckin' wig perfect on her head, immune to strong sunlight and disease. And he'd listened. The effort, getting the words to form, must have destroyed her. He'd listened to the fight in her voice, the labour, defiance, dishonesty.

—Grand, yes. Yes. No, it's great. We're very hopeful. Yes. I'll be dancing again in no time.

He'd wanted to kill her. Really wanted to kill her.

He heard the door now. The boy was home early. He came into the kitchen, saw Pat.

—Oh.

—I'm making tea, said Pat.

—Grand.

—Is that chips you have there?

—Yeah.

—The smell's a killer.

—D'you want some?

—Go on.

They stood beside the table. Pat felt his forehead start to sweat from the heat rising out of the chip bag.

—Good chips.

—Yeah.

Say something, he told himself. Get him to talk. Say something—go on. Speak!

But it was the boy who spoke.

—I miss Mam, he said.

Pat nodded.

—Me too, he said.—Me too.

RODDY DOYLE is an Irish novelist, playwright, and screenwriter and is the author of *The Commitments*, *Paddy Clarke Ha Ha Ha*, which won the Man Booker Prize, and most recently, *Two Pints*.

Jennifer DuBois

The third day in Buenos Aires, out of desperation, Andrew took Anna sightseeing.

At La Recoleta cemetery, they stared at Eva Perón's grave. Its chintzy flowers, its interminable fleur-de-lis, were dizzying in the broad daylight. Nearby, a choir of bleached angels held eternally theatrical poses. Dutifully, Anna snapped a picture.

"Eva Perón was born out of wedlock in the village of Los Toldos in 1919," Andrew announced. He'd printed out the Wikipedia entry and brought it along, for edification. "She was the fourth of five children."

Anna ignored this. "What do you think it's like there?" she said. Off in the distance behind her were smaller trees, stark and terrible as crosses. She didn't take pictures of those.

"It's probably not so bad, Old Sport," said Andrew. He'd started calling Anna "Old Sport" sometime during her adolescence, when it became quietly clear to him that she was his least favorite daughter. "I mean, probably not the Ritz or anything. But probably not so bad."

Andrew fervently hoped that this was true. Lily's holding cell wasn't equipped for long-term detention—there was no exercise yard, no separate quarters for women, and the guards could see her, apparently, when she peed—but then, this wasn't going to be a long-term detention. Compromised privacy was a worthy trade,

Andrew felt, considering what he'd read about the prisons—open sewage, meningitis, prisoners burning themselves in order to get medical attention.

"How are you doing, Old Sport?" Andrew kept forgetting to ask. "Are you hanging in there?"

Anna shrugged. "I'm tired. I'm hot."

"How are you doing, you know, emotionally?"

"I want to see Lily."

"I know you do. I do, too." Andrew was suddenly nauseous, awash with their strange new calamity. There was, of course, no possibility that Lily had actually been involved in any of this. The accusation was so ghastly and so wild and so patently, transparently ludicrous that he'd nearly laughed when he first heard of it. Not that there weren't a few things he could imagine Lily getting justly arrested for. Before she'd left, he and Maureen had had a series of sober conversations with her—mostly about the harshness of Latin American drug laws—and they'd sent her off with an enormous box of Trojans (industrial-sized, Andrew thought, issued for health clinics or music festivals, no doubt). And Andrew had worried about her constantly—he worried about her being kidnapped, trafficked, impregnated, arrested for marijuana use, converted to Catholicism, wooed by a long-lashed man with a Vespa. So when the strangled, half-whispered voice mail from Lily finally came, and the accusation turned out not to be drugs—not drugs, or jumping a turnstile (did Buenos Aires even have a metro?), or trespassing through someone's field while looking at the stars, or any one of the countless thoughtless crimes that he could believe his daughter might have committed—Andrew was mostly relieved. An accusation of murder was outrageous to the point of being comic, and thus was no great threat. Andrew had tried to communicate this to Lily on the telephone, when she'd finally, finally been allowed to call him again. "Don't worry," he'd said over the bad connection. "I know. We all know." Mordantly, from a great distance, she'd said, "Know what?"

Andrew and Anna left the cemetery and Andrew, not ready to return to the hotel, cajoled Anna into going to the modern art museum. They walked with joyless thoroughness through the white rooms—Anna squinting gravely at the art, Andrew squinting gravely at Anna. What, he wondered, would this moment come to mean to her? Maybe it would become merely one episode in her crazy sister's crazy life—something to talk about in bars, on dates, something to tell Lily's own wide-eyed children one day. ("Your mother," Anna might say, "was *wild*.") Maybe this hour at the modern art museum would be merely one of the narrative's many surreal asterisks; something decorative that did not appear in every telling. Or maybe, Andrew thought, this moment would become something else. Maybe Anna would remember it as the very last second that they were still trying to pretend that their whole lives hadn't gone fully to shit.

Maybe she would talk about it in therapy one day—recalling how they'd enacted the self-conscious motions of enjoying the city, as though they were on fucking vacation, and how this was the *exact* kind of pathological WASP repression that had motored them all through everything, always. Which story were they in right now? Andrew wasn't sure he wanted to know.

Suddenly, Anna was on the bench beside him. "You really think it's okay there?"

Andrew nodded vigorously. "I really do think it's okay. Lily said it was okay. She said it was manageable." What she'd actually said was "endurable."

"Dad," said Anna. She looked at him wonderingly. "Don't you know she'll say anything?"

JENNIFER DuBOIS's debut novel, *A Partial History of Lost Causes,* was honored by the National Book Foundation's 5 Under 35 program. This story is an excerpt from her new novel *Cartwheel.*

Geoff Dyer

It's actually very easy to be a man. If you're walking home at night with your woman and she's chilly, lend her your jacket (even if you suggested she bring a cardigan and you've got less body fat and feel the cold more than she does). Do not keep sneakily turning down the heating at home (because, somehow, she feels the cold more than you). Always carry the heavy bags when you're traveling or shopping (even if you have a bad back and shouldn't be lifting anything at all). Do not raise your voice and yell (even if, at her age, she should be able to read a map and know left from right). Do not stand in the hall, jangling keys in your pockets, telling her "We're *already* late" and that she needs to hurry up and get out of the bathroom (even if she said she would be "ready in two minutes" five minutes ago). Do not complain about the fact that there are always long black hairs in the washbasin. (You wouldn't want her to look like a collaborator with a shaved head now, would you?)

GEOFF DYER is a British novelist, critic, and essayist. His most recent book is *Zona: A Book About a Film About a Journey to a Room*.

Ben Fountain

D. Wintermute, corrosion engineer, traversing a two-inch-wide beam in the submarine murk of the Statue of Liberty's cavernous inner shell, wondering how it is that a person could feel claustrophobic in such a monstrously scaled space. So there's that, the shadowy crush of his phobia, plus he's not so fond of heights, either. Outside, the first big storm of the fall is barreling up the Narrows, pounding the Lady with rain and corkscrew gusts. The copper shell knells and echoes, a ponderously dire *thoom thoom* sort of Middle-Earth sound.

"Danny, your situation, please." His boss, Vistap, coming wireless through Wintermute's headset.

"Situation normal, Vistap."

"Then why are you stopping?"

"Well, it's a long way down."

"Redundancies, Danny. You cannot possibly fall."

No doubt. He's swathed in enough trusses and harnesses to supply a lumberjack-themed S&M party. The play of his headlamp along the shell's inner humps and folds makes him dizzy if he turns his head too fast. He creeps along the steel framework looking for crevice corrosion, oxide crust, anything that might explain the rash that's recently bloomed on the Lady's outer skin, in such a strategically sensitive place as to make America the butt of jokes worldwide. The Statue of Liberty has lost her innocence!

This was the joke in its politest form. As the youngest, most agile member of Vistap's team, Wintermute has drawn the task of visual inspection.

Thoom. Thonnngggg. He feels like a bug in a bass drum. He edges all the way out to the Ferralium joints, and spreading his fingertips over the statue's copper skin he can feel rain peppering the other side. He rests for a moment, then spiders laterally along the steel armature, aiming for the general vicinity of the Lady's crotch. The original puddled iron and copper saddles of the armature were replaced twenty years ago by stainless steel. Vistap suspects that annealing the steel during construction degraded its corrosion-resistance properties. But a second theory—and this is the one that excites the careerist ambitions of young Wintermute—posits that changes in the environment are affecting standard materials in new and unforeseen ways. Atmospheric corrosion, higher levels of acid deposition—the possibilities are endless. Then he realizes that while his mind has been musing over the science, the rest of his body has been following his nose.

"Danny, where did you go?" Vistap sounds alarmed.

"I'm just—there's a notch down here, a recess of some kind." He's crouching, shining his flashlight under a fold of the Lady's robe. "Weird. I don't remember this from any of the imaging."

"You're breaking up, Danny. Speak more clearly."

But for the moment Wintermute is too absorbed to speak. He's working the problem, shining his flashlight into the mystery slot, which, Jesus, where does it go? The Lady shifts and creaks, rides the wind with low, persistent moans. A burlap funk emanates from the slot, earthy, peaty, high in iron content. It glistens where his light plays along the lip.

"Vistap, I think I found something."

"Yes, Danny. Go ahead."

"This little scoop or hollow, I think they missed it back in the eighties. It looks like coal tar up there."

In fact his light seems not to penetrate at all. Vistap's answer is garbled, then the signal drops completely. Wintermute is light-headed from the smell, vaguely disgusted, yet intrigued. By crouching as low as possible and bending double he could duck under the lip and have a look inside, but the prospect sends primal shivers down his thighs. He feels queasy. He thinks he might throw up. He wishes somebody else would do this part of the job for him, but there is, obviously, no one else.

Failure of nerve is simply not an option, so suck it up, he tells himself. For the sake of honor, for country. To silence all those jeering foreigners. Be a man, he thinks as he ducks and leans forward, and D. Wintermute, corrosion engineer, plunges headfirst into the breach.

———

BEN FOUNTAIN is the author of the short story collection *Brief Encounters with Che Guevara* and *Billy Lynn's Long Halftime Walk,* which won the National Book Critics Circle Award.

Assaf Gavron

Translated from the Hebrew by Daniella Zamir

The redheaded guy got into my cab without leaving me a choice.
It was in Holon. I dropped someone off in a narrow dead-end alley, the only way out was to drive backwards carefully. I was backing up when I heard a loud bang on the trunk and then he was in my backseat.

I looked in the mirror. It was dark, before dawn, but I could see he was a redhead. And I could see he was huge—a huge head, huge neck, huge arms.

"Where to?" I said.

"Be'er Sheva," he said.

My heart dropped to my balls. Be'er Sheva is a hundred kilometers from here. At least five hundred shekels. Who knows if this behemoth can or wants to pay me such an amount. And the time—I almost finished my shift and wanted to go to sleep. This meant that I wouldn't get to bed for at least two more hours. But to throw him out of my cab I couldn't.

I finished backing up and headed the cab eastward, out of the city.

We rode in silence for two minutes and then I glanced in the mirror. I saw his eyes, looking at me.

"Where in Be'er Sheva?" I asked.

He kept looking at my eyes through the mirror. I shifted my gaze to the road, then back to him.

He said, "Be'er Sheva Prison."

I swallowed. I reached towards the bag of nuts that gets me through night shifts. Shit, empty.

"Be'er Sheva Prison?"

"Be'er Sheva Prison," he confirmed.

We stopped at a red light. I peeked in the mirror again. He was still looking at me with his wide face. "Visiting someone?" I hesitated.

"No. Doing time. Life. For murder."

The red light turned green. I fixed my eyes on the red lights of the car in front of me.

"You're scared?"

"Shitless," I answered quickly. I felt my heart beating in my throat. I swallowed dryly. I didn't have water. Someone once told me that when the end is near, you start to relax. But I wasn't relaxing. The end was near, and I was scared shitless.

"Here, I'll pay you. How much is it to Be'er Sheva?"

"Five hundred."

A rustle, counting, a giant hand in the space between the front seats, tattooed fingers, bills. I took them. I was afraid to count, that he'd think I didn't trust him, so I left the bills in my fist for a long time, and eventually I put them inside a small box next to me.

I turned onto the road heading south. These hours at the end of the night, when the world is almost empty, there's solace in them.

When I looked again in the mirror, he was looking outside his window. I thought that in his gaze there was also solace. I cleared my throat. "Not that it's any of my business," I said, "but if you're doing life in Be'er Sheva, what are you doing in Holon?"

He turned his look from the window back to me. "Prison leave. Forty-eight hours."

I nodded. He continued, with a friendly voice, "I have parole board this morning. They're going to dock a third of my sentence. Eight years, on good behavior."

"Were you good?"

"I think so. I just need to make it on time to the morning lineup, and then I'm set."

I looked at the clock on my dashboard. 05:10 A.M. A pale light began to fracture the darkness. "When's the lineup?" I asked.

"At six," he said.

I looked at the clock again, and then at him again, through the mirror. And again at the clock. Borderline. Did he know it's borderline?

Suddenly, as if he could sense my doubts through the air inside the cab, he asked, "Why, what time is it? We'll make it on time, won't we?"

"Borderline," I told him. And I don't know if I did it by accident or on purpose, but I pulled my foot slightly away from the accelerator, and the speedometer dropped a little.

When I looked up again, there was something different in his eyes.

I thought: He's a murderer. He could kill me and drive off with the cab to the prison to make it on time for the lineup. But it wouldn't be worth it. It would be difficult for him to hide the body and the cab. It wouldn't make sense that on the day of his parole board a prisoner would commit murder. But then again, he's a murderer. Murderers don't operate according to what makes sense or is worthwhile. Or do they?

He still didn't say anything, but in his eyes I saw that he wasn't going to go for the murder option. In his eyes I saw that he knew he was in my hands now.

I stepped on the accelerator.

Assaf Gavron, an Israeli writer, has published five novels, including *Almost Dead,* and has translated various books into Hebrew, including Philip Roth's *Portnoy's Complaint* and J. D. Salinger's *Nine Stories.*

David Gilbert

The kid and I—and he's a nervous kid, wary of crowds, wilts whenever someone raises his voice, like I remember this trip on the subway—I think we were going to a Yankee game though I myself am a lifelong Mets fan, but we had tickets via a friend and the Mets are beyond hopeless and I've been lazy about getting tickets now that Shea is gone, not that Shea was a great stadium but it was a great place to be, or a great place to return to, what with the memories, particularly of Game Six, which is burned in my fourteen-year-old brain, a shame really because it was a crap ending, and the way Buckner slouched right afterwards, the slouch of the future fucked, the slouch of it really happened, my worst nightmare, but we had tickets to the Yankees, and I was pleased because I don't take the kid to as many sporting events as I should, and now the subway is starting to get full, like packed full, and it's loud and it's raucous and it's intimidating, with all that hollering and swearing—my kid hates swearing; he hears swearing and he instantly thinks something bad is about to happen—so I look at my kid, to make sure he's okay, and I can see the tears collecting under his eyes, like a slowly draining drain, something my wife would blame on me and my shaving only once a week, and I can see my son starting to get overwhelmed as we're jostled and jammed, and I have to agree it was nervous making and my dad probably would have muttered something about animals, fucking animals—these fucking animals—but I am steadfastly not my father and I make an effort to treat everyone the same and to understand where people come from, their life, their social norms—my dad would laugh here, loud enough to make you wonder if he was laughing or yelling with questionable cheer—but I want my son to be relaxed in this kind of situation, not to be scared, so I'm telling him, It's all right, they're just goofing around, and I'm smiling and trying to instill in him a little joie de vivre, like the time I hired that mariachi band to follow us around—they were playing in Union Square Park, wearing big sombreros and gaudy outfits, and I was like, These guys are fucking awesome—I said fucking because I want him to get used to swearing, to realize it's no big deal—and I gave them a hundred bucks to follow us around for an hour, and I tell you it was hilarious and people laughed and took pictures, and it was a good time and I think a decent lesson to teach the kid, that fun is out there for the taking even when things seem grim and hopeless, we got sweetly serenaded and that's a bona fide memory, and science has proven that memories are what count though maybe old Bill Buckner would disagree, except Buckner without the error is a forgotten man, that's what I want to teach the kid, that life is hard but you can be harder, and I'm telling him this with my eyes as we stand in that subway, and that's when the fight breaks out between a boy and a girl, both probably sixteen, he was trying to touch her hair and she was slapping his hand away, touch-slap, touch-slap, and the other kids are doing the peanut-gallery routine, the ooooooohs, the damns, and the boy, he refuses to stop, and the girl, she goes all DEFCON 2 and slaps him on the face, I think harder than she expected, and the boy says something truly vile and grabs her by the neck and pushes her into the seats, and now the crowd is no longer a peanut gallery but gamblers shouting their wagers, and it is scary, and it happens so fast, so incredibly fast, and has the potential to quickly get worse, and I can see my kid and he's in such excruciating pain being in the middle of all this and the tears are now flowing though I know he's trying to be brave, which is the saddest part, seeing him trying to be brave yet failing, and I decide that I need to do something, that this is my job as a father, and my heart is a jackhammer busting through concrete as I let go of his hand and push through the seams screaming, Hey, hey, quit it, as though I'm the universal father, and I put my hands on both of them and hope my boldness, however dubious, might stagger them into separate corners, the crazy white man's gambit, and I think I even say, Chill the fuck out, which I instantly regret but in fairness was something I said regularly in college, Chill the fuck out, probably with dudes attached, and the boy and the girl and their friends, they laugh just as you would expect, and for a moment it seems that this is enough, for a moment at least it seems that tensions have been defused—ride on, Number 4 train, ride on, with me its unlikely hero, the good citizen, the noble father, who without that kid staring at me would have slouched into the farthest corner.

———————

David Gilbert is the author of *The Normals* and the new novel *& Sons*.

Alex Gilvarry

got on the train. There were two women of equal distraction. I noticed them in this order. The first had dark hair, Persian eyes, and a red coat with stately buttons. She was all business. The second woman stood by the train door, a yellow scarf on her neck decorated with tiny mustaches. Every aspect of her face seemed to point upward. Right away she gave me a sharp look as if she hated me. So I sat down across from the red coat. This is how I made decisions on the train since I was a kid. The subway is character driven.

I persisted in making eye contact with the first woman. If she were to meet my eyes, I wouldn't turn away. I would hold contact for as long as it lasted. I've seen this done in movies. Beyond that I never knew what to do.

My eyes wandered. I noticed the absence of a ring. Not that a ring has stopped me before. I was involved with someone, presently, who was married to a friend of mine. We weren't such good friends that I attended their wedding, but we weren't just acquaintances either. He worked long hours in the financial district. She worked from home as some type of writer for a women's Web site. I saw her mainly on my lunch hours. The affair took an hour and twenty minutes total, from the time I left my office to the fifteen-minute walk to her apartment at the edge of Grand Street, then back to my office. This included train time. Fifty minutes of the affair was spent in transit. Which left twenty minutes for coitus. It took me two and a half minutes to get dressed, still sweaty from sex. Altogether, it was exciting. I had no expectations. I liked going places.

The woman in the red coat met my eyes. I held the gaze but grew uncomfortable when she didn't turn away. What was I supposed to do next? I smiled. She smiled. I felt pressured by her already so I looked at a poster advertising dental services.

We rode beneath an exceptionally bad neighborhood.

At the next stop, David Grandstaff got on the train. He was a childhood friend of mine. You never forget these people. Grandstaff was dressed in a filthy old army coat. I didn't want to see him. He stood next to the woman with the yellow scarf who was now reading one of the free papers they give out at rush hour. I read the dental advertisement over again.

"Gilvarry," Grandstaff said. He came and pressed my shoulder. "What are you doing on this line?"

"I always take this line."

"How's your mother?"

"She's fine. How's yours?"

"Not so good. I can't really talk. I'm on the job." I knew he had become a cop. His mother had told my mother. "You see this?" He indicated a purple hankie peeking out of his breast pocket. "These are the day's colors. It lets others know who I am so I don't get shot."

"Sounds dangerous."

"Narcotics? You ain't kidding. Last week a guy got shot because he had the wrong colors on. We change colors every day. He's fine, he's alive. It was a mistake. How tall are you now? Stand up."

"I'm six-three," I said without standing up. He was still the same Grandstaff from childhood, a sociopath, only now he carried a gun.

"We were always the same height," he said. "I'm still six-two."

What did he mean "still"? I hadn't seen him since we were young stupid kids. How could he assume we would still be the same height? I knew back then we were different. I stood up out of frustration and he made me turn around so we could stand back-to-back. He patted the top of our heads.

"He's taller," said the woman in red.

"There. See?" I said.

"Yeah, but you have boots on, maybe that's why. I think you're six-two. He has boots on."

I sat back down. "What does it matter?" I said. Grandstaff was interrupting a perfectly good moment between two strangers. There was no reason to play nice. I was no longer young and stupid. I knew things. People were drawn to me, I felt. Women on trains. Small children. This wasn't like childhood. I made my own decisions. I chose where to sit and where to stand. Still, where could I escape to? Grandstaffs popped up everywhere, they were as common as mailboxes. But where were they when you needed to mail something?

Anyway, he got off at the next stop, driven by danger. Something bad would happen to him, I knew it. What if they didn't see his purple handkerchief? What if it blew away in the night? The woman in the red coat looked at me with those Persian eyes. To her, I was now a person of interest.

ALEX GILVARRY is the author of the novel *From the Memoirs of a Non-Enemy Combatant.*

Philip Gourevitch

---

had produced a report about a terribly cruel and corrupt man.

Officially a tax inspector.

In reality an extortionist.

Chiefly a blackmailer.

Also—"As needed," he liked to say—a kneecapper.

And with increasing frequency—such is the fashion here these days—a kidnapper.

But he was just a functionary, and he knew it.

He called himself "a servant of the lower-upper echelons of the Revenue Authority bureaucracy."

He was not being funny.

The self-deprecation was sincere.

He knew no shame, and that made him useful.

I was tempted to write that he was as cynical as he was sinister, but he was not that passionate.

He had decided that his life would be spent making other lives hell, and he was neither boastful nor bitter about that.

He was an impersonal bastard: not a singular crook but, self-consciously, a man of the system that had produced him and protected him, the system that fed off him as he fed off it.

"In this system he serves," I wrote, "everybody is a nobody, and a man who appears to his victims like a fate—all-powerful, inescapable, untouchable—is to his overlords disposable: He was good at what he did precisely because he believed that it had nothing to do with him."

But did I know what that meant?

What was I thinking?

I imagined that by writing about him I was advancing the common good.

The unflinching villainy of this one little shit, I told myself, would unmask a much larger order, and—what?

What did I imagine?

That the system couldn't take it?

I don't like to admit that I was so stupid.

I don't want to accept that I was so vain.

"The abomination of desolation."

I wrote those words from the Bible on a card and taped it over the desk where I typed up my report.

The system took it just fine.

On the day that my report appeared, my man—the tax inspector—disappeared.

My effort did not make his overlords shudder or shrink.

It told them that somebody had to be made an example, and it identified that body.

The tax inspector had once served in the military, and he remained a reservist, so he was convicted and sentenced in a quick, secret trial in a military court.

The offense was "undermining the state."

The penalty was death.

The men who had hired him to steal and to hurt people now held a press conference to decry him as a thief and a thug, and to thank me.

They said how grateful they were that I had pointed out a spot of filth that needed scrubbing.

I had made them look good.

Imagine that.

I felt compelled to write another report.

I said the tax inspector wasn't being punished for his wrong-doing, but for disgracing the bigger wrongdoers.

I said the calculation of those bigger wrongdoers was cold and cynical and yet—this is where I showed I'd wised up—I said that cold, cynical calculation was correct.

I said they had me right where I wanted them.

I said I had set out to teach them a lesson, and they had taught me one.

I said I would never again write a report that could condemn a mere servant to death while his masters toasted their own virtue.

But I wasn't capitulating.

I was declaring my resistance.

I said I would not live by their rules, and I would not keep quiet.

Obviously, I was taking my revenge.

I was putting the finishing touches on my second report when the new man from the Revenue Authority—the man who had filled the vacancy left by my tax inspector—came to see me and said that for the right price my man's life could be spared, and I could be at peace with my conscience.

I was prepared to bribe anyone.

———

PHILIP GOUREVITCH, former editor of *The Paris Review*, has been a staff writer at *The New Yorker* since 1997. His most recent book is *The Ballad of Abu Ghraib*.

Andrew Sean Greer

There are several ways to become a man. Today we will concentrate on the simplest method. Find a man in his natural environment, where he is at ease. A pub or an office can be excellent, as real men feel powerful and relaxed, at their best, and you will have a few to choose from; pick one about two sizes larger than yourself. Height is important. A hotel room is the easiest place to put him to rest, after a few cocktails, but your own home and bathroom can come in handy. You will want him to die with a smile. You will want to leave the genitals intact. It is easiest to begin there and move slowly but forcefully upward, using two fingers for separation, all the way to the chin. Think of an imaginary line where he might button his blue oxford shirt each morning, drowsily before the mirror; when used later, a striped tie can hide any imperfections. From the sternum, bring two lines all the way to the pad of each hand and stop. Below, follow what you imagine as the inner seam of his trousers, perhaps his wedding suit from his first marriage that he still keeps hanging in his closet. Treat the feet and hands the same, but moving around the pad in a question mark. Now it is a simple matter of careful removal of the skin. Find a professional to handle the head. Once finished, you may find a seamstress or, if you are so inclined, work by hand to sew the arms and legs back together. If you're feeling fancy, install an invisible zipper! Again, it is simpler if your subject died with a pleasant expression, perhaps lying naked beside you and smiling at a compliment or a touch of your hand. Perhaps day-dreaming, for a moment, how his life might change because of you. What luck, what luck. A flash into a future of being cared for. A relief from all his struggle, and the father he doesn't like to think about, and the hopes he had for himself as a boy of being rich, rewarded, generous, and kingly. How unfamiliar they seem to him now. That kind of smile. A coating of baby oil can be help-ful at this stage. Now—gently, because after all he deserves it—remove your clothes and climb inside.

ANDREW SEAN GREER is the author of *The Story of a Marriage* and *The Confessions of Max Tivoli*. His new novel is *The Impossible Lives of Greta Wells*.

Mohsin Hamid

———

What did it even mean, walk like a man? Still, Omar was in enough pain to take off his makeup and start trying.

———

Pakistani writer MOHSIN HAMID is the author of *The Reluctant Fundamentalist* and, most recently, *How to Get Filthy Rich in Rising Asia*.

Adam Haslett

The priest listened to the banker weep. The john broke the hustler's neck. The trigger man pulled the trigger. He said, the killer in me is the killer in you. The rapist got away with it. The driver drove. The bartender tried not to hate the kid in the suit. The gamer's thumbs ached. He hated when a game got boring. The dealer pitied his marks. The salesman tried believing. His buddy didn't care. The road warrior missed the flight. Security was all backed up. The front man got nervous. The baker looked for his wife in the ruins. The associate slept at the printers. The CFO got his raise. The liability was covered. The chef got a star. The captain missed the bank shot. The jet mechanic never meant to hit his boyfriend. At the playground, it was all nannies and fathers. The old man had the kid. It sucked to get yelled at.... The janitor admired the view at night but it got lonely. The designer hated the client. The private got a hand job from the colonel's daughter. The writer thought short sentences made him tough. The queen had her day. If the shoe fits, sign on the dotted line. Even if the gig won't last. Make it up. The congressman resigned for better pay. The inmate took yoga to relax. All along the watchtower, cameras kept the view. The drone pilot never drank before the end of his shift. The office was windowless. The officer frisked the kid. The doorman's girlfriend kept saying it would be better if he could cry sometimes about the priest. Winning was the best of all. The sperm count was dropping. The conductor took a bow. The welder's finger was saved. The porn was endless. The actor got shit from friends in high school about being in plays but now he was on TV. The guy washing the dishes sent all his money home. There were no jobs left. The president took one last look at the crowd. The hardship forbearance period was over. The mortgage was huge. During the drought, the farmer stopped reading his Bible. Hooking up was getting old but you could still brag about it for months. The roofer slipped. Marketing got all the money. Logistics was always fucking it up. The roadie's demo went viral. The nurse kept dreaming he was a slave back on a plantation but his wife didn't want to hear it. Time was running out. If it wasn't jealousy, it wasn't love. The trainer kept it positive. No one wants to be a whiner. The shooter's bullets hit the target. Sometimes, it's hard to keep up the act.

ADAM HASLETT is the author of the story collection *You Are Not a Stranger Here* and, most recently, *Union Atlantic*.

Alan Heathcock

Vernon Hamby crouched in his black-walled spear house. He'd sawed a rectangular opening in the ice. The lake water below shone bright and milky. A wood-and-metal fish hung down there. Some time ago a great shadow had passed beneath the decoy. Now Vernon held the spear poised above the hole, intently watching the water, his forearm trembling.

Someone banged on the shack's door. Vernon flinched and his grip failed and the spear sliced down through the icy murk. He eyed the empty depths, huffed a steaming breath, and hoped whoever was at the door would go away.

Another bang.

"*Pastor?*" a woman's voice called.

Vernon considered remaining silent, but she sounded desperate. He stood and found the latch in the darkness. The door opened to sunlight on the lake and hills of snow, a world of blinding brilliance. Vernon shielded his eyes with a glove, squinting to see her.

"Looked long for you," she said. "I need your help, sir."

It was Pearl Ottestad. No more than thirty, she looked old. Vernon followed her across the frozen lake. He knew this was about the fire that had taken their house two nights before. The fire had started in their son's room, the boy left to life support in the county hospital.

Vernon waited until they were in her truck to ask, "How's the child?"

Pearl turned her wounded eyes, shook her head. "Tom's taken it bad. He's gone into the woods with his pistol." She stiffened her chin, grinding her teeth. "Didn't know who to go to. My own husband and he won't talk to me. Didn't know what to do."

They parked near the ruins of the house, charred boards and bricks, trees broken and flame scorched, snow filthy with ash. Vernon lived one hollow over and from his porch he'd seen the fire's orange boil lashing the night.

He asked the direction Tom had gone and Pearl showed him the footprints in the snow. Vernon tracked the prints out through the hickory woods, down a pass and up a ravine, into more trees, leading him to a tiny windowless cabin.

He thought to call out first, but instead pulled open the cabin's door. Daylight slashed into the room. Vernon saw a stock of split wood, an iron stove. The young man sat on the floor, back against the woodpile, the gun on the planks between his outstretched legs.

Vernon stepped in and sat beside Tom. He contemplated Scripture to quote, but none seemed right. It all just seemed like words to him. Pulpit words. Lovely but inadequate.

They sat side by side in silence.

Finally, Vernon said, "I'm sure you know I lost my boy to the war. To a bomb in the road." He closed his eyes, his fists clenched in his coat pockets. "*Be a man*," he said. "That's what they told me after. *Be a man*. A man must be sure of himself. Must stand with conviction. Everybody always saying what they know. What they *know*. That's a man. That's strength. Never afraid, never doubting. *Never, never, never*…" Vernon tipped his head back against the stacked wood, opened his eyes. A crack of darkening sky was visible where the shakes near the peak had crumbled. "Sometimes I wish I wasn't at all a man. I wish I was just a tree 'cause folks can wish a tree to bloom in winter but it doesn't so they don't." He turned to Tom, who stared off toward the iron stove. "We're all just a bunch of liars," Vernon said to him. "Liars and frauds. How much better would the world be if a man just said 'I don't know' instead of pretending like he knows anything."

Then Vernon felt it all anew again, all the pain, the helplessness, and he sobbed and quietly moaned and Tom was crying, too. Shoulders touching, the men wept together in the cold dark cabin.

Dusky light suffused the room. Nothing more to offer, Vernon tenderly gripped Tom's wrist. "I hope I've been a comfort."

Weary, unsure, Vernon left out of the cabin. He didn't look back, hoping with each step not to hear a gunshot. He hid behind a tree and watched the cabin, shivering, praying. At last, sparks burst from the chimney pipe, blue smoke coiling into the heavens.

ALAN HEATHCOCK is the author of the story collection *Volt*. He teaches fiction at Boise State University.

Aleksandar Hemon

Joshua walked home, his buckling prostate quickening his step. He hastily unlocked his front door and went straight for the bathroom, but then noticed the billowing curtains. He was certain he hadn't left any windows open. A deep memory of the way late-night ninjas moved was subsequently activated. Joshua, all flimsy skin and hollow bones, was practically weightless; the dust balls led him, levitating, to his bedroom.

No deep memory was available to help him decide what to do if indeed there was someone in the bedroom. Hence he became instantly paralyzed when he discovered a man kneeling on the floor, weeping, with his face buried in what was, without a shred of a doubt, a pair of boxer shorts patterned with stars and stripes. Joshua had dropped the shorts in the dirty-laundry basket this morning, and there was indeed the basket, pitilessly knocked over, and there was the rest of his dirty underwear lined up on the floor for some perverse inspection. The man's ponytail was tightly pulled back, fluttering in concert with his sobs; he wore a sleeveless denim jacket, so that the tattoo of an eagle with the earth in its talons was blazingly visible on his sinewy biceps. He knew this man, he realized—for a fleeting micromoment, the recognition was soothing.

"Stagger! What the fuck are you doing?"

Stagger leapt to his feet and charged toward the open window, wiping away his tears with Joshua's underwear. He batted the billowing curtains apart and slipped out like a true ninja and the former marine that he was.

Joshua sat down on his bed, gasping for breath, and stared at the boxer shorts array on the floor as if it contained a message to be decoded. His heart was now galloping toward a heart attack. He let out a primally inarticulate scream at the still billowing curtains and got up to shut the window. Before he returned to the bed, he kicked up the boxer shorts tableau. The heart was pounding, the bladder was bloated, but Joshua lay back and looked up at the motionlessly indifferent ceiling fan. Stagger, it might be pertinent to mention, was his landlord and downstairs neighbor. Soon after moving in, Joshua could hear him yelling and screaming, breaking things, slamming doors. One time it had gone on for the entire night, after which Stagger had come up to apologize and ascribe it all to his Iraq trauma. It made him act crazy, he'd said. By way of reconciliation, he'd offered to show Joshua his two samurai swords.

A siren wailed down the street, and Joshua wanted the police to come by; he hoped his mere thought would result in relevant consequence without the intermittent step of his acting it out. He would have watched the ceiling fan till the Messiah came, had his bladder not reached the verge of explosion.

In difficult circumstances, one always finds comfort in the smallest of pleasures and Joshua's urine stream was thick and steady. Above the toilet was a reproduction of a foxhunt painting: red coats and black bubble caps and tall horses and a few clouds bumbling forth over a composed Victorian landscape. Stagger had come up with a nickname for Joshua, who hated it even more than his violent nocturnal orgies. He was going to move out of this fucking place come Monday.

The front door clicked and then something shifted in the corner where the fox was frozen in her escape, all her choices forever foreclosed. The voice Joshua instantly identified as Stagger's said: "What's going on here?"

In a lightning move, Joshua turned, swinging the dick in his trembling hand to spray—from right to left—the upright toilet seat, the toilet paper roll next to it, *A Spinoza Reader* and *The Zombie Encyclopedia,* until, still emitting spurts onto his own thigh, he faced Stagger, who stood akimbo under the hallway light, his face calm and composed to the sharp point of insanity.

"Everything okay, Jonjo?" Stagger asked, and lowered his gaze to grin at Joshua's trickling dick.

He broke out of the bathroom, bouncing off Stagger's flank to fly through the front door, providentially unclosed. He raced down the stairs, not stopping until he found himself in the middle of Magnolia, where he finally returned his penis to its natural habitat. His groin and pant legs were completely wet, his left hand sticky with panic and urine. With his right one he groped for his cell phone to call the police, but then recalled the very motion of dropping the keys and the phone on the front-door table. He rolled up into a squatting pose of pain, but then unrolled like a sped-up footage of fern, because a cab hit the brakes not to run him over. The cabbie, angry and grim as a nightmare, stepped out of the car and said: "Hey!"

That very night, Joshua moved in with Kimiko.

Bosnian-American writer ALEKSANDAR HEMON is the author of *The Lazarus Project,* which won the 2008 National Book Award, and most recently, the essay collection *The Question of Bruno.* He received a MacArthur Foundation fellowship in 2004.

Joe Henry

You couldn't have known.

I was born in 1912 in the south of Montreal to a mother with high ideals and a father dead set on betraying them.

I was set to simple chores: I split wood, killed rabbits, milked cows, shoveled snow, cut ice, and pulled bluefish from black water.

At age nine I was an altar boy. At age ten I was smoking cigarettes behind the parish kitchen, careful not to drop them anywhere but in the cook's tin can that propped open the back door, same as he.

At thirteen I was sent away to a school for the deaf, though I was not; but I spoke little and fluttered my hands as if gifted or deeply troubled. There I was taught to write, dance, sign, add, divide, and conquer. By fifteen I was stoking coke ovens in Hamilton, and a year later tending fire in the engine room of a great warship, steaming out onto the ocean in hopes of making great war. I was homesick and dejected, then taken under wing by an officer intent on teaching me everything he knew while I pulled off his boots and fetched us tea and dry cakes.

By twenty I was running guns for money, and by twenty-three I was giving lectures on infectious disease, pulling down maps and pushing pins in clusters around spoiled river towns. At twenty-eight I was the scandalous beau of a governor's wife, standing always just out of frame in pictures, holding a stack of hats and long coats; and by thirty-one was fighting for my very life against claims that I had lifted certain papers, that might (but didn't) provide our sworn enemies some secret but useless comfort.

I was a sleepwalker, gin rummy enthusiast, stamp forger, dog-sledder, and a would-be chemist who once made a near fatal error on behalf of my own personal pursuit of amnesia. I wrote poems on trains, and once did shadow puppets for children when we were derailed by an avalanche of snow that had dropped like a curtain across the tracks and held us nine days with breathtaking views but little food at the base of a treacherous mountain. I set out alone on foot and brought back help, having been offered free transit for life should I survive.

But that was all a long time ago. I have little that occupies me now, other than the ringing thought that, as you sat in front of me at school so many years back, learning to sign your name into the thin air, learning to read silently moving lips, I might simply have moved my own to say *hear me*—so that you could've read *love me,* and then done so.

JOE HENRY is a musician, songwriter, and Grammy Award–winning producer. Over the past two decades he's worked with artists as varied as Aaron Neville, Bonnie Raitt, Elvis Costello, and Madonna. His most recent album is *Reverie.*

Khaled Hosseini

Mechanic buddy of mine, back in Kandahar, name of Leon—
though his nickname is Mississippi on account of his un-
canny luck with river cards—has this thing he does. For everything
in life, he comes up with a Texas hold 'em analogy. You eavesdrop
on Leon working on a seven-ton and more likely than not he's going on about how so-and-so got slow-rolled by his girl, or how
some guy who'd walked away unscathed from an IED over in
Helmand had hit a one-outer.

If I laid the facts before him now—the hushed phone calls,
the sneaking away in the middle of the day, how distracted she
seems lately—if I asked Leon how solid the odds were Joni was
getting back at me for that brief thing I had last summer when I
was on leave, with that checkout girl at Lowe's, I think he'd say,
Pocket jacks, Wade. At least.

This is what's on my mind now when her cell phone goes off.
I grab it before she can and answer. Some dude on the other end
says he has the wrong number. I say to him, "No you don't. This
is Joni's phone. Who the hell are you?"

He says, "I'm Ray."

"Glad to meet you, Ray." I'm staring Joni down. "Now what is
it you want with the mother of my children?"

Then Joni snatches the phone from me and says, "Hello, Ray.
I apologize for that, I'm deeply embarrassed." She listens, looking

down at her feet. "Yes. Okay. Let me jot it down." She picks up a pencil off the counter. "I'll be there. See you tomorrow. Good night."

After, it seems she's done saying anything to me.

When she tells me, "I found it in the shower," I don't understand at first. "They had me come in a couple times already," she says. "I'm going in tomorrow to get a needle."

She points to her chest and now I do understand, and I start sinking. I let a few moments tick by, collect my thoughts.

"Why didn't you tell me?"

She looks at me like I asked the wrong question.

Later. In the dark. I lie awake, still reeling. My ears ring like they do after a nearby RPG blast. I turn over to face Joni, my wife of ten years, the mother of my three daughters, her hair spilling over the pillow, her profile lit by the moon.

"Do they think it's—?" I can't bring myself to say it.

Joni carries a picture of me in her purse. I'm in uniform, standing collar, white gloves, peaked cap. Seven billion people in the world, most of them perfectly decent, and I'm the lying, two-faced asshole she's chosen to spend her time on this earth with. I catch a flash of her, whip-thin, shuffling down some hallway, pushing a rack with tubing in her arm and a beanie hat on her hairless head.

"Joni," I say. "What am I going to do, if…?"

She sighs. "You're a child, Wade."

The next day, after I walk the girls to school, I sit in the waiting room when the nurse calls Joni's name and I watch a little blue fish in the aquarium swimming in and out of a hollow boulder. One in nine women. I'd read that somewhere. I feel like I can't trust the ground beneath my feet. She looks a little pale when she comes out.

A few days later I'm back on base in Kandahar. I'm sitting outside my tent over at Harvest Falcon, smoking, sweating in 105-degree heat. I've got my laptop on my knees, on the screen an e-mail from Joni. *My Results.*

My knees shake. I haven't had the heart yet.

On my way over from the States, at the Norfolk airport waiting for my rotator flight, I'd walked into a gift shop and looked at the ceramic mugs and the purses and the earrings and the little crystal kittens, and if I had the money, I swear I would have bought her every pretty thing that was in the store. Like that would make up for everything.

I hear the steady thumping of a Chinook overhead, and then it flies past, an ungainly flying RV with rotors. I've been scared plenty in Afghanistan. That one night we drove into an ambush. Taking cover behind an overturned MTVR in the kill zone as rounds crackled next to my head. Tracers whizzing above me, mortar shells bursting all around. But I've never been scared like this. Not like this. I'm terrified to open her e-mail. When she dropped me off at SFO, I said to her, again, *What am I going to do, Joni?* I was thinking of me and the kids, me and the kids without her, thinking of our wedding night, me chugging sparkling wine from a plastic flute glass, watching Joni up on the stage singing "When I Grow Too Old to Dream."

Try being a man, she said flatly.

I sit in the Afghan heat now, looking at the pink-orange haze over the horizon giving way to the dark, and the stars blinking ghostly little dots in the sky, and then I close my eyes and try to remember the words to that song.

Afghan-American writer KHALED HOSSEINI is the author of *The Kite Runner, A Thousand Splendid Suns,* and most recently, *And the Mountains Echoed.*

Bronwen Hruska

This is not your life.

It's not your home or your family or your food. It's not your desk or your state. The bed you sleep in belongs to no one in particular and for the first time in over a decade you don't have to share it. Even the snow outside your window, the tall pines, the river, are not yours. After having lived with your things in your life for so long, it's unsettling. And strangely liberating.

The one thing that is yours here is your time. Twenty-four hours a day, seven days a week. The idea is to write, all day, every day. But in reality all you have to do is, well, whatever you want. And when you put it that way, you start to believe that you actually can. Men have known this for years.

They invented the area code rule. A way to fuck around and have it not count. To contain the chaos of true lawlessness in three digits. You may be beginning to see the beauty in such a theory—in thinking like a man.

Dance Party in the life drawing studio. The words are vaguely familiar. High school. But different. Alcohol and sex—both allowed. There isn't dancing, but there's flirting. And then after too many beers there's kissing on the porch. There's the smell of a neck you don't know but like more than you should. There are fingertips skimming the sensitive skin where your jeans gap in front. There is heavy breathing that makes steam in the cold air that suddenly doesn't feel cold. There is the thrill that someone will see. There is the fear that someone will. There are words. Soft, urgent, thrilling. There are also sounds. Gasps and groans you haven't heard in some time. Anticipation. There is the moment of truth when you have to decide whether to leave the porch and move inside to the bed that you sleep in but is not your own. But you're thinking like a man now and this is not your area code. The decision is surprisingly easy.

Inside, the mood is broken. The lights are bright and your mouth is dry. You slip off the single bed and land on the floor and are too drunk to laugh. You think you ought to call it a night, but here you are, and there he is and you just go ahead and do it anyway. You sleep too late. And then, you realize, there is the dining hall.

Do people know? Do they care? And why are your hands shaking? You see him first. He sees you, then looks away and you do the same. It burns a little, the brush-off. Man up, you tell yourself. Don't let it get to you.

It's distracting, thinking about sex. Your time is now not yours quite so much. You try to write, but you drift back to it. You cringe at the fumbled parts and breathe a little faster at others.

Another party. He dances this time. With someone else. Someone moonfaced and blond. Her skin is pink and scrubbed. The word is wholesome. Young.

You decide to be an adult. Debrief. He agrees to come to the room that you use for the writing you haven't been able to do. To have the talk where you tell him it's over, whatever it is. His eyes are soft. His smile tugs at you. You remember why you kissed him on the porch. There is no touching, nothing to indicate you're ... and then you realize you aren't anything.

A hug as he leaves. His cheek is smooth. The hug slips into a kiss and you're pressed against the wall. Sex through clothes. The best part of high school. Finally you are undressed, skin touching. And afterwards there is whispering and tracing fingertips along limbs and the soft inside of an elbow, a kneecap. Life is good. It's not your life, of course, but here you are, trying it on. And it fits, for now.

You are floating, smiling, humming to yourself, in this life that isn't yours. In the dining hall you're still strangers.

You know you shouldn't do it, but you knock on his door anyway. A long time to answer. He is blurry. Moonfaced girl is curled in his reading chair. She is redder than usual. Will he acknowledge her in the dining hall? That will be the test.

But you remind yourself: There are no rules in this jumble of foreign digits that designate this lawless zone. Jealousy is not relevant. A bruised ego, perhaps. Human nature.

At least you've still got that.

BRONWEN HRUSKA is the author of the novel *Accelerated*.

Marlon James

When me finally dead, only woman should be carrying me coffin. A light grey one with gold trim, but make sure it stay on the cart so that the women only have to push it, not carry it. Watch how you make a girl love you. Call her ugly but say it sweet like brandy coat you tongue—you mean you is a boy and never taste brandy? Call her ugly but sweet and then say, Is a good thing me blind because you smell pretty. Make sure you say she smell pretty so that she ask you what pretty smell like or she going hate you for life. Study your books but don't become no fucking lawyer. Don't tell you mother that I said fucking though you old enough now to hear how real man talk—down there bush up yet? Make sure you kiss the daughter next door so that mummy don't think you're growing up to be a faggot. Don't watch colour TV, let white people stay white, don't watch them turn pink. Learn to cook ackee, or girl will leave the heart inside the fruit and poison you. Learn to cook snapper, or girl will cook a rotten one and poison you. Learn to cook live crab, or girl will cook a dead one and poison you. Learn to wash your shirt but make sure the woman iron it. Don't ever dance the butterfly unless you behind a woman with a big bottom. A boy don't dance alone unless he growing up to be a faggot. You mean you don't kiss a girl yet? How you can have hair growing all sort of place and don't kiss a girl yet? Watch me now, this is how you make a woman put up with you. Leave early, come home late but leave your wallet on the dresser and never count inside it. Watch me now, this is how you keep wife and sweetheart on the same street. Pick a rich wife and a poor sweetheart; they will never discuss you even if they talk every day. Watch me now, this is how you make a boy. Do it on a Sunday, Tuesday, or Thursday, never do it on Monday or you get a girl who grow to be a woman that will spite you. Watch me now, this is how you wear your pants so you don't grow up to be a faggot. Don't talk to no man from foreign or listen when he want to talk to you about books. That man is a battyman and he trying to make you one too. This is what we do to battyman. Smell under me fingernail and you will smell roasting faggot. Don't go to any dance. But if you do go to the dance, make sure it is to meet a girl, and make sure your mother don't know. Go to church once a month for that will make your mother happy. Don't go to the woman down the street for she is every man's girlfriend. But if you do go to the woman down the street make sure you pull out before hallelujah or you going to be a daddy to a whoreson. Don't wear none of those rubber things for that is a plot to kill black people. Don't watch no white people movie. But if you do watch white people movie make sure is Clint Eastwood or John Wayne or Lash LaRue. How you mean no movie star named Lash LaRue? Don't bring no reggae into this house so that you don't turn into a Rastafarian, for that worse than turning into a faggot, but not as bad as turning into a coolie. Don't bring any coolie girl home and hurt your mother heart. There was this man one time, and he was a nice man, but he was an English teacher with only one woman. I hear that his wife say to other woman that men who are that way are the best husbands because he would never have eyes for another woman. You one of them boy who study English?

Jamaican-born MARLON JAMES is the author of *John Crow's Devil* and *The Book of Night Women*, a finalist for the National Book Critics Circle Award.

Bret Anthony Johnston

The woman at the bar had been bitching to the rancher about her husband. The rancher hoped the night would end in the motor court down the highway.

The husband wore tassled shoes and collected coins. He was in Dallas for the weekend, participating in a conference called How to Be a Man. The woman rolled her eyes. She said, "Lessons in archery and Morse code are probably on tap."

"Maybe a seminar on building log cabins. Maybe something on dueling with swords."

"Really it's cigars and drum circles. I picture them bare-chested, reciting Robert Bly."

The night was humid, and the ceiling fans only stirred the heat. The rancher drained his beer, laid down enough money for their tabs. He said, "The Knotty Pine Motel is just up the way. They've got window units."

She smiled, the first time all night, which made the rancher feel younger than he was. She said, "You want to host our own conference? You want me to show you how to be a man?"

"I'd like to relieve you of that dress, I'll admit that," he said.

She nodded and all trace of the smile vanished. She said, "It's too easy."

"Beg pardon?"

"You're all just hairy-legged boys. You're all as gullible as puppies."

The rancher couldn't figure what had gone awry. He set his jaw and put on his hat, feeling jammed up. The bar suddenly seemed smoke-choked, and he was trying to find another angle to work.

"Here's what I'm offering," she said. "I'll roll around with you, but when you slip into those cowboy dreams, I'll clean you out. I'll take your clothes and boots, your wallet and truck and probably some motel toiletries."

"That's about what happened in my divorce," he said.

"You get what you get."

"And if I don't go to sleep?"

"Then we'll go again. Eventually you'll give out. Y'all always do."

"I like my odds," he said.

"Or what if there's no manly conference? What if my husband's here now, waiting to follow us out? What if this is what we do?"

"It sounds like a lot of work for some scuffed boots and an old Ford."

The woman smiled again, stepped off her barstool and shouldered her purse. She said, "You're right, sugar. I'm drunk and nervous. Let's find that motel before we come to our senses."

The woman seemed neither drunk nor nervous, and as they passed through the bar, he wondered if this was a mistake. It would have been easy enough to beg off, but that wasn't in the rancher's nature. He'd see the thing through. In his truck, Waylon was crooning about the basics of love. The woman's hair whipped in the wind and the night smelled of trapped particulate heat, and when headlights flared in the rancher's rearview mirror, he told himself not to worry, told himself it was just another man tracking his way through the dark.

Bret Anthony Johnston, director of creative writing at Harvard University, is the author of *Corpus Christi: Stories* and screenwriter of the documentary *Waiting for Lightning*, about skateboarder Danny Way.

Randall Kenan

Esmerelda Parker McElwaine's first child, born in 1899, they named Tabitha Elsa; a boy child, my great-grandfather, born in 1901, was named, grudgingly, Elihu Increase McElwaine.

They would come to call him Ox.

By the time he was fifteen the young son stood over six feet and would grow six more inches by the time he reached his majority; by his sixteenth birthday he weighed well over 250 pounds—precious little of it fat—so strongly was he built that there could have been no other nickname. Despite his great size the young man had an almost sweet demeanor, quiet, injuriously shy, so withdrawn as if to be ashamed of his gigantism. Stern like his great-grandfather, mysteriously withdrawn like his grandfather, and, like his father, it seemed he harbored some deep inner question upon which he puzzled, some dark central enigma for which he sought some complex and healing answer. Restless, yet oddly calm.

Sometimes for days he seemed to lose the power of speech and would ignore his family members, sitting upon the porch or under the walnut tree; sometimes he would walk off into the woods and not return for a day or more, never explaining, never even mentioning his absence. By and by the family accepted his weirding way—he wasn't hurting anyone after all, they figured.

All seemed well with the towering lad until one autumnal

September evening, during his seventeenth year. There she sat, next to her mother, the legendary Clytemnestra Cross, come to visit her kinfolks. Psyche. All of fourteen. And a half. Her thick mop of black hair—curly and shining in the church light—her lips as delicate as a spider's web, her butterscotch cheeks: The sight ensorcelled the young man to the point that, when the last sermon was ended, and the last offering collected, and the last hymn sung, and folk commenced to socialize and mill about and take their leave, when he tried to speak to her, to say howdy, his tongue clicked and his mouth went as dry as a tobacco barn. But once robbed of her delicious presence, the usually taciturn Elihu McElwaine spoke so long and so much of his vision, his seraphim, that his running mates begged him to hush up.

Clytemnestra Cross and her three children and her husband lived in Asheville in those days, and rarely came to York County, especially considering the brouhaha over her marriage. But Ox would get word about her blessed daughter from one of her cousins. Over a year after that first glimpsing at First Baptist Church, Ox McElwaine took off without a word. At first none gave it a second thought, seeing as how he could go away from time to time. But after a week it became apparent that this time was not like the others.

Six weeks later, he returned with his sixteen-year-old bride.

Perhaps his heart had not yet completely calcified, perhaps looking upon his gargantuan issue, the senior Elihu Increase McElwaine remembered his own young love throes, recognized the thunder of desire, for he quoted the book of Luke: "For this my son was dead, and is alive again; he was lost and is found." And gave his blessing to this new union in the McElwaine clan.

Years went by and Ox seemed to settle down upon his return. By all accounts he grew into a levelheaded, good-natured, dependable, upright man, who did more than his share of work around the farm and helping out others. He sired three children by Psyche, until, one day in 1933, while picking cotton, he stood up, stock-still, and faced the horizon, the sun blazing in his eyes, and he began walking. He was indifferent to the calls at his back ("Ox? Where you going? Ox! What's wrong?"), and looked back not once, and walked till he vanished entirely from view. He was not seen again for thirty-seven years. When he returned in 1970, like a bad omen, he returned as he had left, walking. He walked straight into town, walked his way to the family house, up through the yard, beyond the house, into the wood behind the house, where, after a time, he constructed a small one-room cabin by himself and alone. When anyone was fool enough to inquire as to where he had been, what he had been doing all those years, the old man would simply say: "None of your goddamned business."

Sometimes his granddaughter, Esmerelda, when she was a young girl, would go visit him at his cabin. She liked that she could stay for hours and neither of them speak a word. She liked the silence. She would watch him chop wood, whittle, sit, and smoke his pipe, skin and cook a rabbit. He would cook it with carrots he grew and onions and herbs he found in the woods. The rabbit was good, she said. Never gamey or wild tasting. She never asked him where he had gone, why he had gone, what he had done. But sometimes, she said, while watching him munching on his rabbit bones, she thought she could see it in his eyes, a glimmer, now and again.

What? I would ask. What did you see? In his eyes?

The yonder out there, she said. He brought it back with him.

RANDALL KENAN is the author of *A Visitation of Spirits,
Let the Dead Bury Their Dead,* and most recently, *The
Fire This Time.* He is an associate professor of English
at the University of North Carolina at Chapel Hill.

Etgar Keret

Translated from the Hebrew by Sondra Silverston

My son Lev complains that he never saw me cry. He's seen his mother cry several times, especially when she reads him a story with a sad ending. He once saw his grandmother cry, on his fifth birthday, when he told her that his wish was for her to get well. He even saw his kindergarten teacher cry when she received a phone call telling her that her father had died. I was the only one he's never seen cry. And that whole business makes me uncomfortable.

There are many things parents are supposed to know how to do which I'm not very good at. Lev's kindergarten is full of fathers quick to pull their toolboxes out of their car trunks every time something breaks, and fix swings and water pipes without even working up a sweat. My son's father is the only one who never pulls a toolbox out of his car trunk, because he doesn't own a toolbox or a car. And even if he did, he wouldn't know how to fix anything. You'd expect a father like that—nontechnical, an artist—to at least know how to cry.

"I'm not mad at you for not crying," Lev says, putting his little hand on my arm, as if he feels my discomfort. "I'm just trying to understand why. Why Mom cries and you don't."

I tell Lev that when I was his age, everything made me cry: movies, stories, even life. Every street beggar, run-over cat, and worn-out slipper made me burst into tears. The people around me thought that was a problem, and for my birthday, they brought me a children's book meant to teach kids how not to cry. The book's protagonist cried a lot, till he met an imaginary friend who suggested that every time he felt the tears welling up, he should use them as fuel for something else: singing a song, kicking a ball, doing a little dance. I read that book maybe fifty times, and I practiced doing what it said over and over again, till I was finally so good at not crying that it happened by itself. And now I'm so used to it. I don't know how to stop.

"So when you were a kid," Lev asks, "every time you wanted to cry, you sang instead?"

"No," I admit reluctantly, "I don't know how to sing. So most of the time, when I felt the tears coming, I hit someone instead."

"That's weird," Lev says in a contemplative voice. "I usually hit someone when I'm happy."

This feels like the right moment to go to the fridge and get us both some cheese sticks. We sit in the living room, nibbling quietly. Father and son. Two males. If you were to knock on the door and ask nicely, we'd offer you a cheese stick, but if you did something else instead, something that made us sad or happy, there's a good chance that you'd get roughed up a little.

ETGAR KERET is an Israeli writer and filmmaker. His most recent short story collection is *Suddenly, a Knock on the Door*.

William Kittredge

Snow came early that fall. By mid-December my wife had given up on my betrayals and taken the children off to California. I was living in a cabin beside the Williamson River, feeding dry cows and waiting to get on with life, a lost boy with ambitions, when Oscar, my father, showed up with his new wife, Francis Reynolds, and a yellow Mercedes.

Francis waited in the idling Mercedes, vapor pluming from the tailpipe, and Oscar asked if I had anything to drink. Of course I did, a fine bottle of Jack Daniel's. Then he got down to business. "What are you going to do with yourself?"

This was a reasonable question. My family had just sold our ranching properties. Even after splitting with my wife, I was okay on money for a while. So I told him. I was going to try for a life I'd imagined. Since college I had wanted to be a writer. And now I was thirty-five, I'd driven my family away, and I had funds. So I was going to head for graduate school and see how things turned out. I'd already been admitted at the University of Oregon.

Oscar, an aging rancher given to prodigal excess, looked at me like I'd lost my mind. "Well," he finally said, "I've done things I hated all my life and I sure as hell wouldn't recommend that." So that was that.

We never had that sort of conversation again. After another drink he went down the road with Francis and his Mercedes and I sat there realizing that he'd just let me out of jail. Whatever I planned was okay with him.

Nineteen years later, leaving Phoenix, where I'd wintered, having semi-healed myself and my relations to my children, I headed north to the Willamette Valley where Oscar, eighty-nine years old, was failing in a upscale facility on the rural edge of Eugene. After a good meal and a night in a riverfront hotel, I went to see him the next morning. The nurses had got him dressed, wool shirt and pants, socks and slippers. He was in a small room in a wheelchair, sleeping when I went in. "Oscar," I said, announcing myself, waking him.

He seemed startled. "Bill's coming," he said. Then he grinned. "Who the hell," he said, "did I think you were?"

We laughed and talked for most of an hour, until the nurse came to wheel him away. What did we talk about? Wish I knew. I told him I'd be by to see him the next morning. But I wasn't. I called and told the nurse I couldn't make it. She said Oscar would be sad. Not really, I thought. Well, I thought, he'll last a while. I'll see him this fall. But I didn't. The next morning I was far away.

A week later I got a morning telephone call. Oscar had died in the night. I've regretted that decision—to go play a weekend of golf with friends, leaving him in that care facility—for all the years since. Even while knowing Oscar would not have blamed me a lick. I've learned to consider and reconsider consequences, trying to avoid irrevocable mistakes.

WILLIAM KITTREDGE was born in Oregon in 1932. He's best known for his stories, memoirs, and fiction about the American West, including *Owning It All* and *Hole in the Sky: A Memoir.*

Nick Laird

Hal, there is no trick to it.

The universes overlap in a couple of locations. One is the instant of death, when the man in the eye turns away: The other is conception, when our voices call you from the next room.

Perhaps you have been sitting out there all afternoon watching the bar of shadow slide slowly down the white wall, waiting for your turn. Silently you gather up your things and enter and find the heavy door opens outwards into air, like a hay door high on the side of a barn.

As you fall, you fall out of your clothes, your name, out of your very self.

The fall goes on for so long and is so fast that when you arrive you are clean and slick as an apple pip. There is a bedding down and several months of gyroscopic wetness. Inside your purple caul you bend your head to meet your tail, and that weird beat is your own heart, already counting down.

A change in weather and the flush of light, a wipe and slap to face the world.

Being alive is no small surprise, and this face you'll grow to recognize is yours, sure, but also not. You will look out from it as one might climb to the top of an oak at Tullyhogue and regard Tyrone spread out for miles below.

The place I left when they came for me, I return to visit only rarely. Once, on psilocybin, when the yellow tulips on the coffee table moved their petals like a pout and I lay on the rug and felt the Boundless of Anaximander, how all particles in this world hold each other by the hand, and then last week, when I fainted on the parquet, having jumped up too quickly when you started bawling. I was sure I had gone somewhere since I had to make my own way back, swimming up to surface in my stranger's face again. I held it as a sense memory for days, no details, just an atmosphere of having been necessary and wanted there.

NICK LAIRD is an Irish novelist and poet whose novels include *Glover's Mistake* and *Utterly Monkey*.

Elinor Lipman

My dads set a deadline: Two weeks from today I had to have every thank-you note written. I didn't say, "And if I don't...?" because I'm not that kind of kid. I can't be. So we agree I'll write one at breakfast and two after dinner. And then there was only one left, which was going to the worst asshole in my class, who calls me Cracker because I stupidly told him that our donor egg came from Arkansas. I doubt he even wanted to come to my bar mitzvah, but this is New York City. His Ivy League parents probably said, "You can't *not* go. They'll think you're a homophobe."

I'm not the only kid in my school, not even in my grade, who has two parents of the same sex. As I said before, this is New York City. I pretend it's no big deal, like I'm cool with everything about it. Which was true when I was younger and didn't know how the world worked. But my dads like to go public, and I don't mean on Facebook. I mean *The New York Times* has done human-interest stories on us. First there was the photo essay that shows me getting adopted in court by Pop because Dad is my biological. And they got married last year and I was a double best man, so there we were again. I catch the camera's eye because I have what Pop calls a hardscrabble look. "Not a guy we ever dressed in lederhosen," Dad likes to say. "No Little Lord Fauntleroy," adds one of my two grandfathers, who've been pitching balls at me since I could walk.

Of course we had to go and join the Brooklyn synagogue with the lesbian rabbi. That was fine, but then every kid asks still, "How come you don't go to Temple Emanu-El? It's like two minutes from where you live." I could lie and say, "Tradition. It's where my grandparents got married," or I could tell the truth and say, "Why do we go to *this* one? Surprise, surprise. It's gay friendly. It's in Park Slope, Lesbian Central."

So I have one note left to write. I don't have to lie about liking some dumb gift, because the kids in my class chipped in and got me a pretty big Apple gift certificate, and I was really happy with that. Dad thought I should vary what I say and refer to the kid himself, at the party or in class—not carbon copies like a default thank-you note.

"Can't I just send an e-mail?" I ask.

The two of them look at each other. One finally asks, "What's the real problem, Jake? You're good at this. One more and you're done."

I tell them the truth, not like it's a big deal or the end of the world. It wasn't even big news. I say, "He's the worst."

"Worst what?" they ask.

"You know," I mumble.

Pop says like it's not even a question, "Homophobe."

Dad says—like always, and on some days it makes me laugh— "Do you want us to beat him up? Or his father? Because I can do it with one hand tied behind my back."

He and Pop laugh, but this time I don't. He asks what the little schmendrick's name is and I say, "Wyatt."

Pop says to Dad, "Why don't *we* write it?"

I say, "No! Are you kidding? You wanna get me killed?"

Pop asks, "If you got a note from someone's father, wouldn't it make you feel like you got busted?"

Maybe it would, but I still hated the idea. Not like it was permission, but I asked them what they'd say.

Pop says, "I think Dad and I have been writing this note since your first minute on earth."

I hand over the pen and card. Dad writes and writes; it covers one side then more on the back. I can't look up when he reads it aloud, but I hear, "Wyatt—Thanks for coming to Jake's bar mitzvah. He's getting an iPad with the generous gift certificate. On another topic, please think about this: One day soon enough you'll be an adult and probably a dad. You don't want to look back at who you are now and think, 'I wish I'd never caused anyone any pain, because now that I'm a parent, I cringe at the hurt I might have inflicted.' Sincerely, David & Alan, Jake's parents."

They look so pleased. Their main deal is me. I can't tell them not to send it, or that I'd be paying for it. I add a stamp, and on the way to hell, I mail it.

ELINOR LIPMAN is the author of ten novels, a short story collection, and *I Can't Complain: (All Too) Personal Essays.*

Vanessa Manko

I t is done with the body, not with the mind. She should feel when you begin to move and if she precipitates the wrong direction, you've done something wrong. Then, it is your job to guide her. That is your role. If you are precise and certain, there will be no confusion, no hesitancy. You must approach it with a will. She will sense you, feel you, and follow. But you must not look down. To look down is to break the contract, to give up on the agreed rules and parameters. Instead, you intuit. Sometimes it just flows. No plans. Nothing. Just an ease. Other times there is resistance and so it will take a little more doing, as the man, to assert direction. But you must be clear and commit to the left or right with decisive action. It's best not to talk. A few words exchanged, maybe, but nothing more. You aren't there to make friends, exactly. You must concentrate, but not too much otherwise your body will not perform the way you'd like it to. If you think too much, she will pick up on it and lose confidence in your abilities.

Once, I gave the nod to a woman. She acknowledged me and stood up. We began almost instantly. It all worked. No knots or messy configurations. No false starts or tripped up, misunderstood intentions. We went on like that for a while. A few times around. Everything going smoothly until, without any warning, she pulled away from me, said, "Thank you," brightly, with a polite, endearing smile that did not imply what, to my mind, the "thank you" meant—an end, no more, me relegated to watch her with other men until she left and I never saw her again. Later, I learned from a friend of hers that she was new to the whole scene, hadn't yet learned the etiquette, mainly that "thank you" is generally understood as a dreaded cutoff, almost akin to a rebuff of your initial, invitational nod. But, well, that's how it goes. In life you plan, plan, plan, but with the tango you just never know.

VANESSA MANKO is a former dancer with the Charleston Ballet Theatre and dance editor of the *Brooklyn Rail*. Her writing has appeared in *Granta*.

Ayana Mathis

The customers weren't supposed to drink at the Bonne Nuit. Yeah sure, there were the ones who ordered those virgin mai tais but most came in with the job already done, if you know what I mean. And then there were some who brought their own, and the bouncers pretended not to see. But tell me this: How could you miss a silver flask sticking halfway out a back pocket? I'm talking about one fella in particular, always liquor-leaning against the catwalk when I did my twirl. Never tipped and fell asleep between acts. Never said much either, that is until the bouncers hustled him out the door, him waving that flask around, "Babylon can't bring me down! I got me! I always got me." Why they kept letting him in is beyond me. I saw him one night on Royal with a wool cap pulled down over his ears. I tried to go the other way but he was quick-sighted for a drunk. He told me this story about how some people stole a car and inside the car was a woman and a baby, and instead of making the lady get out these people—I don't know, I guess maybe they got spooked or were high or God knows what—these people shot the lady and the baby too. "What kind of world . . . ?" is what the drunk fella said and I said that was a reasonable question he was asking. I wish now I had said something better, but to tell the truth it was chilly and I didn't want to talk about something so unnatural as shooting a baby, and plus I was on my way home. But this fella, this regular at the Bonne

Nuit, he kept saying, "They shot the little bitty baby." He was so torn up about it I wondered if it could be him that shot the baby, or maybe he was the baby's father. "How am I supposed to draw another breath in this ugly world?" He was swaying on his heels all right, and that flask was glinting under the streetlight. The top was loose and I was going to tell him but I didn't want to get any deeper in the conversation and I thought, which is stupid, I know, but I thought if the top came off he would have to throw the flask away and then maybe he would stop drinking. He had pretty eyes, kind of green-blue. Then he said, "Am I supposed to take revenge?" And I said, "For who?" "For who? For who?" he says. "The baby, of course!" And I said the baby was gone, wasn't any revenge to take that would matter. I was feeling the chill in the air, all around my ankles. I think a fog was coming. There's nothing lonelier than feeling a damp chill late at night on a street corner with a fog coming in. He said, "I believe if I did take revenge God would be with me in the barrel of my gun." I'm not naive. After all, I had just come from seven hours at the Bonne Nuit—I see all kinds. But I can tell you that man was... Well, I thought maybe he had heard that story a long time ago and it was knocking around his head for years and maybe he had been trying to figure out why this and why that and that's how he ended up swaying and swerving on the corner of Royal and Canal with that liquor stink coming off his skin. He must have had a big heart for it to be hurt so bad. If I had a man like that, a man that could feel something so much, he was changed by it... I mean, what if I had never met this fella at the Bonne Nuit because he didn't go there and I didn't work there, and what if he was a stand-up type guy? Well now, that would be some kind of man. Of course, he wasn't that kind of man, and it was late so I gave him a cigarette and five dollars and walked on home.

AYANA MATHIS is the author of *The Twelve Tribes of Hattie,* which was recently selected for Oprah's Book Club.

Colum McCann

M an the fuck up. Give me back my dead girl. That's all I'm asking. I sit here every day, staring out. Got a front porch. Got a metal chair. I don't get drunk and I don't stay sober. I aint keen on getting high. I just sit here, thinking backwards. It's a long way home. I watched her coffin get carried through the church. They played the saxophone the length of Tupelo, turned the corner and went down Burgundy. I didn't want no folded flag. I didn't want no military taps. I aint saying I was the best, but I weren't the worst either. She was mine. Blood and eyelid. I used to give her baths. She sat down in the little bitty bit of water. I scrubbed her back. She said, Auntie. All childy about the soap in her eye. I put her hair in braids. She say, Quit tugging. She a mouthy little bitch sometimes. I say, Listen to me. She says, No. Thirteen, she's out climbing trees. Fourteen, she's running with the boys. Fifteen, she driving along Urquhart. When the hurricane came, she went out and stole a popcorn maker. A popcorn maker! Only thing left on the shelves. Never even used it, not once. Left it sitting on the kitchen counter. She say, Fuck this shit, I'm bored. Eighteen, she walked out the door. She sent letters back. Fort Hood. Kandahar. She manned the fuck up. That's what she did. Cleaned her rifle. Shined her boots. Walked out under the starry shot-up night. A land mine, what it was. She flew out through the windshield. That

shit bulletproofed supposedly. She out in the middle of nowhere. When she hit she skidded along the dust. She lying in a patch of ground like she been slapped from the sky. Just orphaned out there. Steering wheel beside her. Black and round in the dust. Bits and pieces of tire. Metal twisted. Sunning down hard yellow. She already lost her leg. Everyone else dead round her. Bits and pieces. She better off quick dead herself. She hear a truck coming. She's hoping it's a helicopter with a shot of morphine. Or maybe that shadow will be a stretcher. Maybe that moaning belongs to a guitar. But that aint no flower of dust. That aint no recognizable shoe. They stand there with their gun barrels pointing down. She stared up at them. She said, Shoot me. They took their turns instead. They manned up.

(Once on Royal I saw a flatbacker in a station wagon with a sign on the top that said $10, a line round the corner to Montegut, waiting, she was spread out wide in the back of the car, I guess they were manning the fuck up then too.)

Floods is the word they use, but they should call it something else, like remembering maybe. The Sergeant came knocking on my door. Up the steps past the watermark. Ma'am, he says. I already knew it, gut instinct. He sits there. Ma'am this, Ma'am that, Ma'am the other. He says, Ma'am you mind if we turn off the television? And I says, Don't matter none to me. So I turn it off. We sit there. That's what we do. He's looking at her photo. She's gone dolphin. Swimming in my eyes. Your niece did this. Your niece did that. I'm just staring at him. Listening to him from the bottom of the sea. I drifted out to the kitchen. Slid my slippers along the dry floor. I put on the popcorn maker. Plugged it in. I hit the button. The corn goes *pop pop pop*. I wait. It blooms out all white and fluffy. He's still talking at me, but I'm in the kitchen just listening to that pop pop popping. He says Ma'am, can you hear me? And I say, Yes,

sir I can hear you. And I'm thinking, Man or woman, it don't matter, you get blown in the air, you aint gonna come down any fuller.

———

Colum McCann is the author of the National Book Award–winning *Let the Great World Spin*. His new novel is *TransAtlantic*.

Ian McEwan

Don't turn away from me," his wife is saying. "Don't look away. Don't you dare. Look at me. Look at me!"

When at last Sebastian slowly turns his head towards her, their eyes lock. His are wide, scared, bluish black, and below them is a swag of aubergine, a crescent on the pale and frightened young skin.

She says, "We're eight floors up. More than a hundred feet. If you jump, you die!"

How could he not know that? Is she trying to tempt him? He's on a ledge, she's on the roof, safely behind a parapet, a retaining wall.

The ledge is less than eight inches wide and he's obliged to keep his feet turned to the side. Below him to his right is the window he climbed through ten minutes before. Filling the window, leaning out her large head and the black curls she refuses to have cut, is the woman he was making love to twenty minutes before. Her head is level with his knees. He can't bear to look down at her.

The woman who is his wife is on the roof, gazing at him across the hypotenuse formed by a corner of the building. This line of sight is a geometrical abstraction suspended in space above the car park asphalt far below. Whereas he's a living thing, a vibrant entity, a sack of blood, a failure.

How did he make such a mess of his life, how has he managed to be so creative? His existence is in such chaos and he's just beginning to grasp a new fact—he doesn't dare die.

Here's the list: Jasmine, his wife, is chronically disabled and ill and says she can't live without him. His lover, Maria, is eight weeks pregnant by him. Her husband, Tony the plumber, in his thick-headed way half suspects the affair. Two days ago, Sebastian was sacked from his job on the ticket counter at the railway station after an argument with a customer. He's overdrawn at the bank. His wife has nothing beyond her disability allowance. Maria too has nothing of her own.

Sebastian can't leave things like this. He can't afford it. And wanting suddenly to live makes him frightened that he might die, and looking across and up at his wife does not help.

She could throw him off with her furious eyes, she could knock him down with an insult.

She's getting her first good look at the woman he loves. For all the insistence on looking into her eyes, her own gaze keeps switching down to the destroyer of her marriage. She sees a head of curls framed in metal and peeling paintwork. Like a portrait in the Museum of Modern Art.

Or perhaps she suspects nothing. Perhaps she thinks he's suicidal on account of being sacked.

But she must be wondering how he came to climb out through that woman's window.

He crawled out here because he heard a knock at the front door. He thought Maria's husband had returned early from work without his key. Tony would pulp his skull with a wrench.

But it was only a fellow come to read the electricity meter.

And now that Sebastian is on the ledge, he's lost his nerve and can't see how to bend down and climb back through the bathroom window. A goodwilled neighbour must have seen him standing out here and phoned down to his wife on the third floor.

Jasmine suffers from back pain nearly all the time, and a rare kind of arthritis in her knees, so that sex in any disposition of limbs is agony for her. And though she's pretty, pain has made her a scold. She's seven years older than him, they've been married two years. She talks to him like a child, bosses him about, complains about him with a bitterness that demoralises him and binds him to her with guilt.

For six months he was dreaming of escape.

He opened a secret account and put away £15 a week. His idea was to save for an airfare—to the States or Australia—and for £500 in cash. He was going to leave Jasmine everything—his apartment, his car for her to sell, and a letter telling her that they would never make each other happy.

And he would be gone forever.

Then he met Maria from the eighth floor, and then she was pregnant and he's had to give her all his secret savings. His guilt has bound him tighter to his wife.

Now he's a hundred feet up and, just to clarify matters, Maria's head has been replaced by Tony's.

The plumber is indeed back from work. He's reaching a powerful hand around Sebastian's ankle and beginning to shake him loose from the ledge.

What to do? Sebastian sees the car park far below. So many Škodas! From under his shoe, a piece of masonry falls away from the ledge. Three seconds later he hears it hit the ground. He hears Maria scream, begging Tony to be merciful. What to do? He thinks he knows.

I'll phone my editor.

The phone is in his pocket, the number is in the chip.

"Yup."

"Frank, I'm in a mess. I'm only two pages in and a hundred feet up and already I've got five characters including an offstage meter reader, and a sacking, and chronic, acute back pain, an adulterous affair, a pregnancy, a furious wife, a crumbling ledge with a lethal drop, a murderous plumber with a wrench. It's all too much. I'm dizzy. I can't go on."

"You must go on."

"But Frank. It's a hopeless mess, a worthless melodrama. Everyone will hate me. I'm failing, I'm falling...."

"You must go on."

"You don't understand. It's already a failure. A ridiculous set piece. I've aimed too high. A hundred feet! I can't go..."

"You must go on. Sebastian, be a man."

"Frank, I can't go on.... I ... no ... yes, I'll go on."

IAN MCEWAN was born in Aldershot, England, in 1948. He is the author of *Atonement, Amsterdam,* which won the Man Booker Prize, and most recently, *Sweet Tooth,* among other books.

Patrick McGrath

Boris Roscoe showed up at Rikers Island and bailed his mother out of jail. She was then living on the fifth floor of a walk-up between Second and Bowery. She hadn't finished a painting in months. She was fifty-seven years old and since the day Boris's father kicked her out, her journey had not been easy. But she and Boris and Boris's sister, Willy, who lived in Ibiza, had clung together, in a sporadic kind of a way. Few enough people understood the weird bond they shared. They didn't understand it themselves.

When Boris saw her in the bail office she was wearing a headscarf with a crowfoot pattern on it, like an old-time convict uniform. Some kind of a joke, he guessed. Her mood was far from playful however. The indomitable, the fearless, the *fearsome* Joan Roscoe had suffered serious damage in Rikers, and was weaker than Boris would ever have thought possible.

—Oh Ma, he said.

He got her back to the Bowery in a cab. When they were in the apartment he gazed at her and was at once aware of warm pressure behind his eyes. Boris Roscoe was an emotional man. He'd always found it hard to hide his feelings, and had almost made a bad scene in the bail office. That was exhaustion in part. Now he saw this strong, stubborn woman he'd admired and feared all his life brought low, made small, by the small-minded bullies of the criminal justice system of the City of New York, and it moved him to tears of pity and rage.

—Oh for Christ's sake, Boris, don't start *weeping*.

She touched his face, frowning. She then went over to a record player on a plank supported by bricks and dropped the needle on a disc that must have been waiting on the turntable a month at least. Prokofiev, one of the haunted sonatas, the one about the wind in the graveyard. It was scratchy but it didn't matter. Joan sat at the table opposite Boris, her head in her hands, at one point reaching out without lifting her eyes to touch her son's damp cheek. On the table stood a bottle of wine. She started to talk. Some of her troubles she laid at the door of a man called Baranski but he wasn't the real problem. No, her work was the real problem: Her confidence was shot. This was how all the trouble started.

She sat there nodding her head.

To the wall was stapled a square piece of canvas cut from sailcloth. On it was sketched in crayon a rough outline of the Chrysler Building, visible from the north-facing windows of the apartment.

—Why not just go up to it and—

Boris stood up and made some dramatic painting gestures in the air. He was a tall, stout, shaggy young man in a poncho, with leather sandals on his sockless feet. It was still bitterly cold in New York and he clutched his wine in fingerless wool mittens, hoping it would keep him awake. He'd been traveling for three days without sleep and considered it faintly heroic that he was sitting in this freezing flat having with some difficulty rescued his mother from Rikers; and as to why she'd fetched up there, he knew this much, that she'd assaulted a man in a bar who turned out to be an off-duty cop.

She continued to talk in a meandering fashion, pushing her glass back and forth across the table. Then she turned and stared out the window, where the Chrysler Building was like a jeweled dagger in the night. The haunted violin whined and scraped.

—Look, I just can't start.

—You *can*!

—Don't humor me, Boris.

They sat in silence. Boris saw the first fingers of dawn claw the eastern sky. Then he told her what his sister Willy had suggested, and saw the sudden quick lift of interest it aroused. He told her Willy's island offered long days of warm sunshine, she could breathe there, and more important, work. He said her painting would be full of light again.

—You think so, do you?

—Yes, Ma, I do.

—I'm not going to some fucking convent—

—Just *shut up*, said Boris.

For once in her life she did as he told her. He said they weren't asking her to move into a convent—

—You say that—

—Just come to the Mediterranean with me.

This time she listened. It was the word "Mediterranean." To her it meant light. She took a drink of wine and ran her tongue around her teeth.

—Boris, you got any money?

—Ma, I'll get the money.

So it was decided.

———

PATRICK McGRATH, a British novelist, is the author of *Spider, Asylum,* and most recently, *Constance.*

Jon McGregor

———

We knew it was getting close when they asked whether we'd thought about how to say good-bye.

There had been seminars. Guest speakers had come in and shared their experiences. Some of them had broken down as they spoke, gripping the lectern. Usually the military men. The scientists and the rest seemed to have a firmer hold of themselves. A certain detachment. They spent a lot more time talking about what they'd done while they'd been away, rather than how they'd found it hard to adjust. But the pattern didn't always hold.

The worst was this one man who'd tried to unicycle around the world. He'd had his wheel stolen in Kazakhstan, and it had taken him longer to get out of the country than he'd planned on taking for the entire trip. He was going around doing these seminars called Failure Can Be Your Gateway to Success but it didn't seem to be working out. When he got to the bit about keeping in touch with loved ones back home, he put up a slide of his wife and children and turned round to look at it and just stopped talking altogether. His shoulders were shaking, and he held out a hand to ask for a moment. The moment went on for a really long time. His wife was pretty good-looking and the kids looked full of beans and the question some of us were thinking while we waited for him to regain his composure was why you'd go unicycling around the world if you had a family like that. Next thing we knew he was gathering up his papers and unplugging his laptop and striding towards the door. The speakers made this really loud humming noise after he unplugged the laptop. He had to come back for the unicycle saddle, which he'd brought along as a visual aid.

A staff sergeant who'd served in Iraq told us about the way younger soldiers had become addicted to their smartphones and video chats towards the end of the mission there. He talked about how the traditional thing was to wait for regular letters and parcels, to line up at the pay phone once a month, but to mostly focus your attention on the job in hand and your colleagues on the base. He said the problem with the increased connectivity was that the younger soldiers never quite left their home life at home. This was a distraction, he said, and a dangerous one. Better to leave home behind and then when you get back you'll all be pleased to see each other again. The second thing I do when I get home to my wife is take my pack off, he said, and he looked surprised when we didn't all roar with laughter.

Obviously no one had explained the nature of our mission to him.

The seminars were a bit pointless in that way. None of these people had any idea. Some of them had been away from their family for months, while people died in unexpected ways every day and everything they ate tasted of sand. Some of them had rowed around the world, eating and sleeping in a box no bigger than a coffin, not speaking to anyone for weeks at a time. Some of them had lived in shacks on the Antarctic Peninsula while the sun stayed below the horizon for months and the snow piled up over the roof. But all of them, by definition of the fact that they were standing in front of us in this seminar room, had come back. All of them had planned on coming home. So what could they tell us?

The advice given was that video and audio contact would be significantly restricted and would in any case not be possible after the first seventeen hundred days. The suggestion was made that such contact would be undesirable from a psychological point of view. It was recommended that departure sessions be held in person, in private, on a given date before moving to mission-readiness.

Chief gave us a briefing. He talked like someone who'd been working on his lines for a while. He said, There will be no easy way of doing this, but that's what being a man is all about. He said, You're going to have to take a deep breath and say the kind of good-bye that very few people ever have to say. You're going to have to stand up straight when you walk out of that room. Those of you with children, they're going to want you to show them how to be a man. Do yourself a favour and show them right.

Then he packed up his papers and went home and a group of us went round to the loading bays and found some old plywood packing cases to kick the shit out of.

Jon McGregor is a British novelist. He is the author of *If Nobody Speaks of Remarkable Things* and, most recently, the story collection *This Isn't the Sort of Thing That Happens to Someone Like You.*

Antonio Monda

M y son doesn't speak to me. I know he loves me, that's without saying, and I know that he loves me especially when he tells me that he hates me, that I don't know anything about him, and that he has nothing, absolutely nothing, in common with me.

I also know that this is the age in which sons don't talk with their fathers, and they attack them with violence, make fun of them, are ashamed of them, and humiliate them. In other words, they kill them.

I know all of these things, because I have read a few books, but above all, because I did the same thing to my father. Seems like yesterday.

But then, my father died at the time when I was insulting him and making fun of him, and I never had a chance to reconcile. I ask myself if it was fate or God who decided that it should be this way. And I also ask myself if his sudden good-bye wasn't possibly his way of responding to me.

In any case, I carry within myself this torment since the last day in which my father tried to talk to me, and then again the next morning when they made me see him, lying on the bed dressed in a blue suit and rosary in hand, ready for the coffin.

Until the evening before, I had done everything contrary to what he said, and I did it in a way that he would be fully aware of my actions: It was my way of communicating, of becoming an adult, but now I curse that language.

It has always been like that since the beginning of time. I certainly don't believe that I can change the way in which men become men, but I ask myself why love needs conflict. Why must it disguise itself with hate. Why should it bring pain.

I would like to tell my son that he is making me suffer. And that he must talk to me, because I do know well this language he has adopted, but I have wanted to forget.

I would like to tell him that when I try to talk to him I am attempting to explain how to become a man. Because this is what a father must do, and this is the language of my age.

I ask myself if to love means to find the precise language.

But then I think that perhaps I must become a man as well. And perhaps the reality is that we never become men.

ANTONIO MONDA is an Italian journalist, screenwriter, director, and author. He is an associate professor at NYU Tisch's Kanbar Institute of Film and Television.

Robert Mooney

Halloween, and we had the doorbell fixed like a family might fix a cat and the front lights turned off as if my father weren't home and me beside him with a book in my lap. Weak lamplight cast shadows in the room. Knocking at the door argued the silence back into itself. Before leaving for Mass with my sister, my mother had glared at my suitcase blocking the door, said something about supper on the way home, set her eyes on me hard, and turned away.

I kept watch alone. He'd been in a coma for three days on a hospice bed where the couch used to be, where he would sit in the evening after dinner and try to tell my future, the *Times-Union* folded on the cushion beside him. We shared the same height, the same blood, but his voice was gentler, his eyes a lighter blue, his life clearer, his hair darker—thick as fleece, cropped close to the scalp. Years ago he'd forsaken the patch of toupee for the side where his hair didn't come back. It must have been a bother pasting it on every day. He'd comb the top hair down over it, but it never covered the spot completely and, not yet a man, I'd feel embarrassed to be with him.

His hands were yellow on the sheet where my shadow fell. An IV tube nourished his dying. A snore tearing the air gave hope, as it had long ago when, lying in my bed across the dark house, I would follow his breathing like sheep to a wide-open dream. On my lap was the Jerusalem Bible. I don't know why this of all the books in the room, maybe because it was the largest, open and ready on the credenza. Maybe because stories you already know comfort more than the ones you don't. I had been reading for a half hour but was only to where Eve, tempted, tempts Adam. I kept looking up to listen to the wind, or the chants of the angry children outside, or his breathing. I wanted to whisper something in his ear but was afraid.

Cain murdered Abel, the waters assuaged for Noah, Babel went up, God tormented Abraham at Moriah. I looked to the darkest corner—not because of the noise but the silence: no wind, no children, nothing. His mouth was an O: dry, tight, a hole in a white face I'd shaved that afternoon. I stopped breathing too. He began a breath with a gag and stopped. I slapped him with the front of my hand. I don't know why. His head had turned on the pillow and I slapped him again, hard. For a long time I waited, staring into his mouth. I waited until tears rolled down his cheeks from my eyes.

The number of the Anthony Funeral Parlor had been posted on the wall by the phone. I don't remember dialing, but there was a knock heavier than any child could make. Two men in long coats stood in the wind. Somebody had written CUNT in shaving cream under the knocker. The old man introduced his son, who was taller, his hair brushed back with tonic. They came in as though entering a church.

Both struggled him into the kind of plastic bag an instrument might be carried in: gray with white trim. At one point his hand fell and struck the floor. The old man, glancing at me, tucked it back curtly into the bag. It had a zipper. They carried him out as if in procession, the bag hitting furniture, the doorjamb. I followed through toward the hearse parked in our driveway. Skeletons and mutants and witches stood near, rattling trick-or-treat bags, conspiring. They watched the men lay the bag into the hearse. I wondered if I should go with him but I just stood there as the men got into the front seat and drove away. Red taillights blazed at the corner and vanished into the dark. White breath from my mouth hung like vinegar on the air.

Voices of children sounded far off. Wretches circled, chanting, *Why didn't you answer? Thought you weren't home! Thought you weren't home!* laughing and rattling and pointing. Something splattered on the driveway at my foot. I grabbed a skeleton's bony arms and shook it. Its skull looked plastic under the moon. I wanted to snap those bones, crush them in my hands, but the arms were warm, resistant, trembling. He wasn't a skeleton, only a child, somebody's son.

"You *fucker,*" I said. "That was my father."

Robert Mooney teaches creative writing at Washington College. He is the author of *Father of the Man.*

Liz Moore

McCluskey had her by her ankles and Ames had her by her wrists. Jim was in charge of the camera.

Get this, get this, said McCluskey to Jim, and he and Ames lifted her up from the floor and swung her gently back and forth, as if they were two parents, almost, swinging a child. Her head hung back and her hair swept the ground.

Holy shit, said McCluskey. Are you getting this?

There were times that night that Jim wondered if she was dead, but every so often she opened her eyes partway and mumbled something, almost in a whisper—twice she said something about homework and once about dogs, and each time she was smiling. They laughed.

Weekend at Bernie's 2, said McCluskey, and then left her alone for a while on Schiffman's pilled and grubby couch.

Jim walked from one room to another. A boy from the basketball team gave him a hard slap on his back and said *Jimmy!* as if in surprise. It was his first time drinking. It was the first time anyone had invited him out.

Later in the night when Ames and Lewis were drunk and bored, they pulled her pants and underwear down to her ankles and Jim looked away at first, it was so close, he had not seen one before, except on a screen. But they told him to get it so he did. He took the picture and then looked at the picture on his phone, which felt better than looking directly at her.

She was pretty in school. She was bad. She took any pill she could get. She was in Jim's classes but didn't know his name. She'd gotten with McCluskey. She'd gotten with Ames. She was called slutty by people who would know. She was not liked by girls. She did not speak to teachers, even when called upon. Jim liked her. He had for a while. He stared at her in class and in the hallways. He knew what her hair smelled like. He knew what color she was wearing any given day. He knew her middle name because he'd seen it in the yearbook.

Now he made himself look at her. Her skin was very white. There were small red bumps where a razor had taken her hair away. There were red rutted lines where the elastic bands of her underwear had pressed into her skin. The pink parts of her were thin and wrinkled and delicate, as delicate as paper, he had not known.

McCluskey was the first to put something in her. A beer bottle. Get this, he told Jim, and he did. Ames found a pen and put that in her too. Jim watched her face. She never moved. Everyone crowded around her and put their hands near her, pointing to the pen and the bottle, the bottle and pen. Jim took a picture of that too without being asked. He left out their faces.

Text those to me, said McCluskey at the end of the night, and he did.

Later, once the pictures were posted, he thought of animals: a pig, a frog, an insect. He thought of something dissected. He thought of a humiliation of his own: the time he pissed himself at Boy Scout camp, and how that had felt. He remembered the warmth as it made its way down his leg, his dim horror in the seconds before anyone noticed. He thought of prisoners—the frightening hooded prisoners in photographs that Mr. Colgan, his favorite teacher, had projected onto the whiteboard in his political science class last fall. The prisoners were from one place and they had been taken to another. One was naked and wearing a dog collar. One had his hands extended out like Jesus on the cross. What is it that the soldiers were trying to teach them? Mr. Colgan had asked his students, but nobody could say.

LIZ MOORE is a writer and musician. Her novels include *The Words of Every Song* and *Heft*.

Dina Nayeri

When I was a boy, a newly arrived exile in Oklahoma, there was an incident that scorched me for months, dwarfing all the urgent memories that surrounded it. So much is forgotten now in comparison.

We started going to church a few weeks after moving to Sitting Bird apartments, our shabby corner of this new country. Baba and I dusted off our best clothes, faded brown suits we had worn on the plane ride from Iran. My sister, Nasreen, put on a pink frilly frock she had worn on the first day of school. Maman wore a dark funeral dress and Baba brushed his mustache. We were so terribly mismatched. During the service Pastor Clark made a big show of introducing us to the congregation. He talked of the miracle of our escape, the joy of working with the underground Iranian church, the heavenly reward for those who help their brethren, the situation in Iran. I looked around the tired Sunday-morning faces, trying to find kids from school. I recognized a few from the playground, smiling blond boys with their hair gelled back. As I stared, I lost track of the pastor's words, snapping to attention only when I heard Baba stammer beside me.

"Yes, my brother," he began, his eyes nervous, his hands hanging between his thighs, cycling through his green counting beads at triple the normal pace. The pastor must have asked him some unexpected question. "Let me see ... is long story. I think is not worth so much your time," he chuckled, cleared his throat. "But as you say, many blessings. We leave Iran in rush and without certain where we live." He kept stopping, hoping that would be enough. But the pastor continued nodding and urging him on. I cringed at all the many eyes fixed on my family, on me, and on my father, the once joyful bard whom I had never seen fumble through a story so clumsily, so humbly. "There was refugee camp. A blessing. And then here, praise Lord, with you good people."

Throughout this speech I stared at my hands, picking at my cuticles and comparing the brownness of my skin with the woman sitting to my right. I wished Baba would stop. I wished I knew what was expected in an American church—though we all saw by this point that church had a different meaning here, where there was no threat of death and sometimes people came not because they yearned or believed. Here, Baba had earned no respect; even his degrees were useless. He was no longer the same man and he mentioned it at every opportunity. "Soon I take USMLE exam," he said, "is needed to practice again." The skeptical glances from all around drove my gaze into my lap. I didn't dare look up. When the collection plate came around, men and women dropped bills and coins, passing the plate quickly to the next person. But Baba rested the plate on his lap, fumbled in his pocket, and then—to my horror—made change, dropping a five and picking out three ones. I wanted to say, *No, Baba, this is wrong.* But I didn't and I felt like a coward for it. When he passed the plate to me, he smiled, and I saw a bit of the old pride—of being a benefactor of the church—faded, but still in there somewhere.

Decades after that day, I can still see Baba, his feet planted on the crimson carpet of the sanctuary, making change in the collection plate. I watched him do this and I felt like a coward for saying nothing. Now I'm thankful for whatever force kept me silent...because fuck anyone who would judge a man for being poor.

There are dark tunnels that the well-placed never see, all the struggling that happens just below their feet, just below their upward gaze. Everywhere, the poor live by rules that they make for themselves. And everything about them is in how they got there.

DINA NAYERI is an Iranian-American author. Her debut novel is *A Teaspoon of Earth and Sea*.

Téa Obreht

At dawn, take note of the missing. It will seem as if they have gone on ahead, but you already know you will never see them again. Like those you have come across broken and sundered in the grass, they do not come back. Because their absence is nameless, the weight of it will walk with you until their faces and voices fade. Wait for those spared to gather in the clearing. Understand that today you, too, were spared.

Cover ground before the sun is at its highest. Move from shade to shade, water to water. Keep the young always within your sight, or in the arms of their mothers. Listen for every sudden flush of sound in the grass. Stop sometimes, look back for the missing. Wonder what keeps you looking when you have already learned they are not here, not anywhere. They are nowhere at all.

When you pass other wanderers on the plain, keep your distance. Wonder what happens to their kind, whether they, too, ask themselves about the outer darkness into which the missing disappear.

Long for the missing. When the first story comes to you at sundown, think of them. When you tell it, give them names.

Téa Obreht is the author of *The Tiger's Wife*, which won the Orange Prize and was a finalist for the National Book Award.

Edna O'Brien

———

Open the heart valve. Read some great female writers, from the two Emilys—Brontë and Dickinson—to present day. Tell me that you sometimes dream as you did when you were a child and spake as a child. And yes: bring home the bacon.

———

Irish novelist, poet, and playwright EDNA O'BRIEN was born in 1930. She is the author of more than a dozen books, most recently, *Country Girl: A Memoir.*

Joseph O'Connor

In the year I turned sixteen, I had a summer job washing dishes at a local restaurant, in our hometown of Montauk, Long Island. My father had run away with his girlfriend the previous Christmas, and there was a strange tolerance in the house as a result. When the summer came to an end and I returned to school, my mother, who was by then a very serious and religiously disturbed alcoholic, allowed me to keep the job as an after-class activity. I liked going to work at the restaurant.

The back door of the kitchen led to a car park where the chef and I smoked weed or passed time with the construction workers who were demolishing the old motel across the lot. I had a little sideline going, by which I would sell them booze I'd stolen from the storeroom, occasionally a box of frozen chicken breasts. The chef didn't mind. He was a tolerant Albanian, and for 50 percent you could persuade him to be staring hard at his pots as you hefted a crate through the kitchen. Who knows how he came to be boiling lobsters in Montauk, Long Island? Probably it hadn't been his boyhood dream, but I never got around to asking him.

The construction workers were mainly Irishmen, talking of places I hadn't heard about, in a collegial, backslapping, conspiratorial way. Like all Irishmen I have known, they were sardonic in humour and assumed you gave a single damn for Ireland and her people. They enjoyed mocking me for not having a girlfriend. In time, it began to annoy me. Even the Albanian was joining in. And while I wasn't in any position to insult them by way of self-defence or vengeance, I could see that I would have to do something.

So, spurred by their barbs, I asked a girl out. Her name was Verity Moore. She was beautiful, bright, witty, vivacious, with cheekbones you could hang a hat on and the ability to speak French. She was an accomplished musician, grade six at the dulcimer. She was also learning the clarinet, progressing nicely. Verity Moore was one of the loveliest girls in all of Long Island, several degrees out of my league. Like me, she was aged sixteen but was sensible and calm. Her father, who disapproved of me, was an orthodontist in Amagansett, a remarkable thing to have achieved given that he looked like the porn actor Ron Jeremy.

I spent every spare evening with Verity, and every spare hour of the weekend. Back at the construction site, I would regale the now silenced and awestruck Irishmen with juicily redacted tales of our dates. The movies we had seen. The romantic strolls on Ditch Plains beach. The night before Christmas, when she kissed me.

How sweetly we remember the first kiss of our lives. When mine happened, the world seemed to stop turning. I felt I could reach out and stir the stars around in the sky. I explained to those Irishmen that Verity Moore's kiss was like none other. I wanted to them to be envious, and they were.

I didn't reveal to the Irishmen that my angel didn't exist, that I had invented her out of scraps of movies and overheard conversations just to give myself something to tell them. Nor did I confess that this particular form of kissing had never happened to me, and that kissing of any sort at all had been a fairly limited thing in my life. I had kissed elderly relatives, usually under duress, mainly because my mother had assured me that I'd be mentioned in their wills if I did so. A former Roman Catholic, I must surely have kissed a crucifix, although, oddly, I don't remember that now. Certainly, I had kissed the poster of the punk singer Debbie Harry that glowered with low-lidded sultriness over my virginal bed. In the photograph, she was wearing a Sex Pistols T-shirt and torn, low-slung leather jeans that revealed, with shattering eroticism, about a quarter inch of her panties. Had you been there yourself, you'd have kissed that poster. I kissed my way almost through to the wallpaper.

Finally came the night when I told them Verity and I had gotten it on. They were rapt as I gave out the details. Obviously, I had to improvise. And that wasn't easy. The only person I had ever been to bed with was myself, a person I was sometimes fond of, whose sense of modesty I admired, but the sex could be a bit, well, meh. I was beginning to get the feeling that myself and I would be better just as friends. But we were finding it hard to split up. Still, those Irishmen didn't seem to suspect the truth. If they did, they said nothing about it.

The lights on Gosman's Dock were as nothing to the loveliness of her eyes, the electric power of her kiss. The bricklayers would ask me, "How are you and Verity getting along?" I would tell them, "Mind your own business," or "Fuck off back to Dublin," which abuses the Albanian found amusing.

In my life I've had sexier sex, or sex that meant more, but I'm not sure I've had sex that could ever compare with my first, despite the fact that it was a work of fiction. She was a wonderful lover. And I'll tell you the truth. I don't think I'm over her, even now.

She cost me two marriages, that waterfront beauty. I wonder what she's doing these days. A man is by definition a person capable of being his own audience. It's a thing I learned while young among the lobsters; gazing at the streetlights of Montauk, Long Island, and wishing they looked more like stars.

Joseph O'Connor is an Irish writer known for his novel *Star of the Sea*.

Mary O'Malley

I t's like this," he said. "She's a complete hoor."

"Oh now, Mairtin," she said.

"Did you hear she put in for a divorce for herself?"

"I heard that alright."

"And do you know she got it?" He looked ready to cry.

"And the kideens too?"

"I heard something alright. I'm sorry it went that way."

"Divorce." He sounded bewildered, as if the word were in Swahili, or Dutch.

She said nothing more. There was no use talking to him. He only did what all belonging to him did. His own mother wouldn't fault him. He worked twelve-hour days on Chicago building sites and bought a house. Now his wife was telling him to go, turning him out like a dog. Telling him when he could see his own kids.

He talked to Ann because she was from home but she wasn't hard. Ice got into some of the women from home when they lived in America and they got that hard glassy look that no man could get past.

Ann talked to him because she saw him in the pub late, breaking his heart over something he couldn't fix and couldn't understand. And because when they first came over and things were hard in '92, Mairtin left a thousand dollars in their kitchen in an envelope and his only response to their thanks was "Sure it's only dollars. Monopoly money. Oh when I was going over the Cork and Kerry mountains…"

"The kids will be fine," she told him.

That she was divorced herself, from his friend and sometime boss Sean, didn't enter into it.

"Do you know what the bitch said to the judge? She told him I tried to strangle her. He asked me did I. I said—"

Ann laughed. "Ah Mairtin, she did not. That's an awful thing to say."

"She did."

"And what did you say?"

"I said I did not. He said it was my word against hers.

"Anyways, if I was going to strangle her, she'd be strangled, not lying through her teeth in an American court.

"Then they said I'd have to make an appointment to see my own kids, like going to the dentist, and I said I wished I did strangle her. The bitch."

He half laughed. She hoped he had more sense than that, but with Mairtin, you could never be sure.

"What'll I tell them at home? What'll I tell Mamai?" he asked so quietly, she hardly made it out. His accent got stronger under the pressure of emotion.

"Tell them it didn't work out," she said. "That's all. It happens."

She stood and touched his shoulder briefly.

"Was it true?"

"Was what true?"

"Did you get rough with her?"

He looked at her like a spaniel.

"Ah sure, things got a bit out of hand sometimes after a night out. You know yourself."

She knew alright. Maire said it only happened when he drank. It was like a switch went in his head.

"There's no real harm in him." That was what Maire told her, at the same table, crying. "He's like a big child."

"Can they do that, Ann, with the kids?"

"Mairtin," she said kindly, "they can."

Going past him to make more tea, she thought of all the men she knew that were like big children and wondered why there were so many and why so many were bewildered by life and by women and the crooked ways of love.

As she came in with a fresh white pot and put it on the table.

"Fair play to you Ann a mhac," he said. "You make a great pot of tea."

"Look Mairtin, if there's anything...," but he'd turned away and started singing:

"He's lost his faloorum, faliddle aye oorum,

"He's lost his faloorum, faliddle dal day...," and she sat and poured, and waited until it was safe for him to stop singing and turn around and drink his tea.

MARY O'MALLEY is an Irish poet. Her latest collection is *Valparaiso*.

Michael Parker

———

When he was in high school, the boy took a job in the afternoons and on weekends at a drugstore. The alcoholic pharmacist yelled at him for things like being sixteen and not knowing how to back a trailer or put water in a car battery. He could not squeegee the windows worth a damn, and the one time he was allowed to run the register, it came up just shy a dollar. Go clean the items in the window, the pharmacist said to him one afternoon, and the boy took a dust rag to the wheelchairs, canes, walkers, and other medical supplies staged on the platform by the plate glass. The arrangement of the items bothered him, for he was prone to moving the furniture around in his bedroom every few months so that he could walk into the room and feel like he'd never been in it before or that it belonged to someone else, someone with vision and options. Once he even took the sliding doors off his closet and pushed the head of his bed against the wall, and he did not even mind when he woke in the night to a nightmare of jungle and vine, only to realize he was being grazed by the cuffs of his Sunday trousers. Lying in bed among belts and neckties hanging from coat hangers made him feel he was living in a city, in an apartment so small he had no choice but to put his bed in a closet, far from his parents and the pharmacist. He wanted to transform the window of the drugstore into something similarly fresh and disorienting, but there wasn't much to work with. It wasn't fully possible to arrange the merchandise in such a way that did not say to people on the street, Not only are you going to die, but we are going to make some money off your demise. But in order to create the opposite emotion he felt when he woke with his head in a closet, he would have to leave everything the way it was, the way it had been since he'd taken this job, probably since the drugstore first opened its doors. And now the boy felt stuck: He did not like the pharmacist and he did not want him to make money at all, much less profit off of the elderly and infirm, but leaving things the way they were, depriving the world of the spark of renewal, seemed to him equally distasteful. And so, seized with an anxiety that produced in him not jitters but lassitude, he sat down in a wheelchair to try and to think what to do. The pharmacist must have been either busy or drinking with his buddies in the stockroom, for an hour passed and the boy sat undisturbed in the wheelchair, struggling with the confusion of his desires as outside people passed by without a glance his way. And he hated them for it, and he loved them for it, too.

Michael Parker is the author of five novels, most recently, *The Watery Part of the World,* and two short story collections. He teaches writing at the University of North Carolina at Greensboro.

Benjamin Percy

He is only a boy. But when he whimpers home from school with a split lip and pouched blue-black eye, his father tells him to stop crying. He is weak, his father says. Don't be weak. That night the boy stands naked in front of the mirror and hates what he sees, the hairless delicacy of his body, the weakness evident in it. He shaves his head and glues the hair to his chest and armpits. He drinks gasoline and swallows a match to burn away the highness of his voice. He slits his arms—and shoves stones into the slits—rounding his biceps. He cracks open his thighs and his calves and grafts them onto 2x4s to lengthen them. He cuts off his little cock with a long knife that he then houses in the freshly rendered cavity. And when, the next morning, he clomps down the hall for breakfast, a bowl of fruity flakes and a short glass of milk, his father claps him proudly on the back while his mother weeps and says she does not recognize him.

BENJAMIN PERCY, a contributing editor at *Esquire,* is the author of *The Wilding* and, most recently, *Red Moon.*

Jason Porter

———

Here is me. Fourteen. Skateboard. Nervous complexion. Attention pills. Plan to destroy earth unless I can get a girl to kiss me before the end of the year. Here are three things: mouth guard, trumpet, video game. Here are four things: breath mints, tube socks, firecracker, throwing star. Here are six things: crumpled tissue, lingerie catalog, headphones, sunglasses, regular glasses, secret book about anatomy. Here is one thing: a photo of a father and a son sitting on a bench, their hair very similar, their noses very similar, bored by each other. Here is one more thing: Here is one last thing: The earth is already destroyed.

———

JASON PORTER is the author of the forthcoming *Why Are You So Sad?*

Ron Rash

I t's a drearisome day," Uncle Earl said, hunching his jean jacket tighter around his shoulders, "but maybe it'll clear up before the service tomorrow."

I looked out the windshield and figured otherwise. Fog could stay in our valley for days. It was like the mountains circling us poured the fog in and set a kettle lid on top. That grayness came seeping through the walls and into the house too. Bright things like a quilt or button jar lost color and footsteps sounded lonesome.

The road curved and the Tilsons' farmhouse appeared. A car was parked beside Mr. Tilson's blue pickup.

"That's Preacher Winn's car," Daddy said. "Probably best just to go on to the field."

Daddy eased the truck onto the far side of the road and we got out. Uncle Earl took the butcher knives and sacks from the truck bed and we walked down the slope and through a harvested cornfield, damp stalks and shucks slippery under our feet. The cabbage patch was beside the creek. Two of the rows had been cut but four hadn't.

Uncle Earl nodded towards the field across the road. The fog was thicker here in the bottomland and it took a few seconds to see the tractor. It lay on its side, one big black wheel raised up, the harrow's tines like long fingers.

"He shouldn't have been on a hill that steep," Uncle Earl said.

"No," Daddy said. "But I've known many a man that least-ways had a chance to learn from that same mistake."

They set down the sacks and kneeled at two row ends.

"Stay between us," Daddy said to me. "We'll cut and you sack."

They began cutting, left hand on the cabbage head while the butcher knife chopped underneath.

"We'll be filthy as hogs by the time we finish," Uncle Earl said, brushing wet dirt off his overalls.

"Try to keep your clothes clean, son," Daddy said. "I got need for you to do something else when we finish."

"At least as clean as a ten-year-old boy can stay," Uncle Earl said.

I dragged the sack behind me up the row, having to tug harder every time I put another cabbage inside. Daddy and Uncle Earl stopped every little while to help catch me up. Soon as one sack got full I'd run and get another and start filling it. After a while I heard the car at the farmhouse drive away. We didn't trifle but it still took two hours.

"Fifteen full sacks," Uncle Earl said when he and Daddy had loaded the last one in the truck bed. "You still of a mind to take it to Lenoir today?"

"Yes," Daddy said, "but I need to ask her if she wants some for canning."

"Then we better go see," Uncle Earl said. "The preacher's gone, so it's likely as good a time as there'll be."

We walked across the road and into the yard, where Daddy and Uncle Earl stopped.

"Take your shoes and socks off," Daddy told me. "Then go up there and knock."

I did what he said and went up on the porch.

Mrs. Tilson opened the door. She had on a black dress and I

could tell she'd been crying. She looked at me like she didn't know who I was, then fixed her eyes on Daddy and Uncle Earl, who stood in the yard with their hands in their front pockets.

"We cut the rest of the cabbage, Faye," Daddy said. "We didn't know if you wanted to keep any for canning. If you do, we'll put it in the root cellar for you."

Mrs. Tilson put her hands over her eyes, held them there. Then, real slow, she let her hands rub hard against her skin, like she was pulling off a mask to see better.

"Sell it," she said. "That's what Alec always does. Done."

"We'll do that then," Daddy said. "We'll see you at the funeral tomorrow but if there's anything you need done before that, let us know."

Mrs. Tilson didn't say anything or even nod. She just stepped back inside and shut the door.

"Mrs. Tilson, she's grateful to you for helping out," Daddy said when we got back in the truck. "She may never say that though. It's a hard time for her and she'll likely not want to ponder anything about these days.

"Anyway," Daddy said as he cranked the engine. "You done good."

Ron Rash is the author of numerous books, including *Serena* and, most recently, *Nothing Gold Can Stay: Stories*. He teaches at Western Carolina University.

Salman Rushdie

In my dream there were white wolves in a tree. He, the great analyst, told me I must have seen my parents having sex doggy fashion. I was afraid of the white wolves in the tree. He told me I must have seen animals having sex and had imagined my parents doing it that way. I told him I couldn't open my bowels. He told me it was all about sex. His colleague said I had been sexually abused as a child.

My sister committed suicide. My father committed suicide. I suffered from depression. The great analyst analysed me and said that I was cured.

After that I tried to be a man who could bear his burdens as a man should. I tried not to be afraid and to shit normally. It didn't work. So I told people the great analyst was wrong, wrong about the white wolves, the doggy-fashion sex, everything. Nobody understood what I was saying.

The great analyst died and I was not cured. I was just as unwell as before. The enemies of the great analyst said he had been wrong about me, but nobody was right about me, not even myself. My bowels did not open without enemas. I was filled with fear.

This is what it has been for me, manhood. When I look at myself in a mirror now, I am sure I see a third hole in my nose. I am sure that, when I wasn't looking, the great analyst drilled an extra nostril into my nose. That was his idea of curing me. He is dead but the hole in my nose remains, at least in the mirror. In my dreams there are no more white wolves, but the great analyst is there, telling me the third nostril means I am afraid of castration, I have a complex about castration, he says, I think someone is going to castrate me.

The great analyst is wrong. I don't think about castration. I hardly ever think about my penis at all. I never think about sex, which doesn't appear to be for people like me. Another great analyst says my sickness has nothing to do with doggy fashion. He says the wolves are all my different selves.

So I am a schizophrenic now.

I had a dream about an angel who wanted to become a man so that he could taste food and touch women and be in love. I wanted to say to the angel, Don't do it. Stay up there on the architecture and don't come down. If you come down, somebody will tell you your problem has to do with doggy-fashion sex or castration. Somebody, when you're not looking, may drill a hole in your nose.

I had a dream about a girl who was really a man and who was happy after she had the operation and wanted to play baseball with other men. I could not understand the girl, who spoke a language unknown to me. It may have been Spanish.

I had a dream about a dog turned by an operation into a man, with a man's brain and testicles. The dog behaved shockingly as a man, was vulgar, lewd, violent. I thought the dog-man must have had a dream about a tree full of naked white men. I thought maybe the dog saw his dog parents having sex like men, in the missionary position, and was traumatized.

I don't understand any of this. I am a part of the *this* that I don't understand, and so is everyone who couldn't understand me. To be understood, I have sometimes thought, would have been a cure. To have someone say, *I understand,* and for that to be true.

Finally, inevitably, I died. I don't know what that meant, either, but it solved a few problems.

SALMAN RUSHDIE is the author of eleven novels, including *The Satanic Verses* and the Booker Prize–winning *Midnight's Children*. His most recent book is *Joseph Anton: A Memoir.*

John Burnham Schwartz

There is this: One day he goes with his parents to visit his great-grandmother at her "home." His parents make him. He has been there before. The home which is not a home. The home with nurses who themselves look like old, sick people; where the food trays and piss jugs are made of blue plastic; where the walls have the calcified shine of bones. The smells make him gag, or think about gagging. Granny sits in a wheelchair in the one corner of her room that does not get the sun. She is dressed in wool, even though it is very hot outside. His parents speak in quiet voices for a while, and then his mother reaches into her purse and pulls out his recorder. "Play for Granny," she says. He knows the rest. He puts the recorder to his lips and begins to play "Danny Boy" for his granny because she is so old that she has lost her sight and can only listen, and the only thing she has ever wanted to listen to in his presence is "Danny Boy." When he is finished playing, he hands the recorder back to his mother and she returns it to her purse. There are tears in the desiccated folds of his granny's face. He kisses her, tasting salt, smelling death, and then he goes out. In the hallway there is an old woman lying on a movable bed, a mostly naked man with an aluminum walker, and a younger couple who are hugging each other and whispering. The smell is powdered urine. He walks quickly until he is outside, where he takes deep breaths of the clean air and feels the sun on his face.

He sits down to wait on a low brick wall to the left of the electric door. For a while, he is calm. He feels as if he has escaped, and the sun is very warm on his skin. In his head he hears the sound of the notes he played for his granny, the lingering, terribly sad sound of the song. Then the song is over, and he is still waiting for his parents to come out. His mind is drying up. He tries to remember his granny's face, but the longer he sits there in the sunshine and clean air, the harder it is for him to see her. Finally, he gets to his feet. Above him on the wall of the home is a small red box which says ALARM.

When the firemen come, he will still be there. And he will still be there when the old people are evacuated on their wheelchairs and gurneys, their IVs and oxygen tanks trailing behind them. A death march. No, he's not going anywhere. He did not do this to hide. He did it because he never liked "Danny Boy." Not ever.

JOHN BURNHAM SCHWARTZ is the author of *Reservation Road, Bicycle Days,* and most recently, *Northwest Corner.*

Mona Simpson

'll tell you how to be a man. Stop doing every single thing you're doing and have been doing, that's first up. Stop it. And stay still. Close up your shop. Shut your eyes, ears, nose especially. That mouth too. Don't eat nothing. And most of all, turn off that faucet where all the charm spills out of, splashing over every person you ever met, women of all size, shape, and color and some men who ask, is he gay, really? Really? He seems kinda gay. You got to find a new way ALTOGETHER. Make time for the frenzy to die down, the sham obligations to fall away, the phone ringing, the computer shining its lights, the device making its noise that only means someone on an unlimited plan zapped you—that took less than a second and cost them nothing extra. Just begin: Think of the most amazing science fiction world that could ever exist; that's that another person, someone you know, anyone, me even, imagine she is real. With a back end as intricate and crammed with wires crossing as yours.

That will make the earth tilt.

MONA SIMPSON is the author of *Anywhere but Here, Off Keck Road,* and most recently, *My Hollywood.*

Jessica Soffer

First

Meet her at the flower farm. Meet her when you're high. Meet her as you're staring at the fifteen varieties of purple plants and her voice is kind and firm. "Those ones smell amazing," she says, "but they won't last."

Take her to dinner. Take her to concerts that she will enjoy more than you. Take her to meet your friends and take it to heart when their wives whisper that she's perfect.

Let her cook for your father. Let her knit him a scarf. Let him be sweeter than he ever was to you, or your mother. "He is so lost without her," she says, washing your father's dishes, missing the point.

Wish that she understood grief. Wish that you didn't. Wish that you'd known to ask your mother if she was happy all those years, or if she would rather have been alone.

Marry her because her genes are not riddled with depression. Marry her because you make her unlonely. Marry her because you don't believe that anyone will love you more than she does.

Stay with her because of the kids. Stay with her because she shuts her eyes when you kiss. Stay with her because on your twentieth anniversary, she will look at you like she still believes.

Forgive her because she never turned you on. Forgive her because your children do not see the world as you do. Forgive her because she let you be. And she forgave you.

Second

Again at the flower farm. Meet her as she's staring at those purple plants, hands in fists, and you realize how long you've been waiting for something like violence.

Meet her as your wife is nearby, organizing and reorganizing the receipts in her purse. Meet her when it feels like you've stopped making memories, when it's too late for something like this.

Take her to the woods where she screams threats into the trees. Take her to the cabin where you get drunk and honest. Take her to the ocean where you talk to your mother, and watch her take off her clothes in October and swim. Take her.

Take her again.

Let her tell you the truth about yourself. Let her be the reason you run, photograph, tell your father what you really think. Let her make memories and make everything hurt more, hurt less.

Wish fear could stop you. Wish it was only about risk. Wish you wanted to take your wife to that BBQ place, that country, that abandoned house with all the windows. Wish you knew which was worst: to be her, or *her*, or you. Wish you knew what your mother would say. Wish you could stop with all the goddamn wishing.

Don't marry her because of the kids. Don't marry her because it cannot possibly last and what if it did. Don't marry her because no one who has ever understood you has been able to love you still.

Leave her because she cannot stop telling you who you really are. Leave her because you cannot stop believing her. Leave her because it is too much. It is too much.

Forgive yourself because you always wanted a family. Forgive yourself because you've come this far. Forgive yourself because you lost your mother before you could ask her about hope: how much is reasonable, how much is too much.

Third
Meet her.

JESSICA SOFFER is the author of *Tomorrow There Will Be Apricots*. She teaches fiction at Connecticut College.

Rob Spillman

Attend an all-male mid-Atlantic high school. Girls, the alien other, are walled off in all-female schools just down the road. A year younger than your classmates, you overhear all the things your classmates claim they've done to the mysterious, unknowable girls. Before high school, you lived with your gay musician father, your reality the opera stage and the diva swirl around it. Your new classmates are lacrosse-playing gods, scooping up the walled-offed nymphs like the entitled deities they are. Long for their manliness, their certainty, their privilege. They will rule this minor city and you will run far away and spend the rest of your life trying to unlearn how to be a man.

ROB SPILLMAN is the editor of *Tin House*.

Matt Sumell

M—

I've done a lot of things in my time I'm sorry about (a lot), *and for all the many, many bullshit excuses, I've always had the stupidity of youth to fall back on. I could always tell myself:* It's okay. I'm young. I'll get it. *I don't have that anymore. Maybe that's why this fuckup's got me more fucked-up than usual, or maybe it's my mother's dying words:* "Don't hurt ladies." *Maybe it's the effects of prolonged drinking or the effects of the short intense variety, but my guess is it's all of them plus this:*

You're really important to me. I'm such an idiot. Here's some flowers. See you Thursday.

Love,
M.

P.S. I don't know if you can believe it, but somehow getting punched, twice—and I probably could've used a third—was exactly right in that it triggers a particular flash of brain-lightning that penetrates the fog just long enough to see the horizon and change course. I don't know if that makes sense—I stole it from Emerson, I think—and even if it does, I can't promise I'll stay on it, but for now anyway I feel better about where I'm headed. So thanks for clocking me.

MATT SUMELL is currently finishing his first story collection, *Making Nice*.

Manil Suri

Krish tries to cheer me up each time I get depressed. "It could be much worse—you could have been reborn as an ant. Do you know how many lifetimes it would have taken just to reach this level then?" He goes on to explain karma yet once more. "Depends on your previous sins, but it's really a game. Look at me, for instance. Reduced to a dog like you, and I didn't even kill. But to whom can one complain?"

I prefer not to dwell on what I did in my last life. An accident, not murder, I still maintain. In any case, nobody deserves an existence like this. Living on the streets, subsisting on scraps. Looking for a lamppost each time I need to relieve myself. Itching so bad, I want to scratch off my skin.

It would have been better if they'd erased my memory banks. The house I owned, the life I had. Gliding around in a chauffeur-driven sedan. And women!—how nice they tasted, how sweet they smelled. Now sniffing myself is the only fun I seem to have. I'm tired of being a dog, I want to be a man.

"Who doesn't?" Krish says. He reminds me it depends on how much good I accomplish. "Everything you do, you get plus or minus points. A stray would be lucky to come back purebred. To jump any higher, you'd have to score pretty big."

The problem is there's limited opportunity for good deeds in a canine existence. You only encounter damsels in distress if you happen to be Lassie or Rin Tin Tin. The most I've managed to do is rescue a chicken from a trash bin. Which doesn't even count, because it was cooked and already dead, Krish says.

He tells me my time will come—I just need to look out for it. Sure enough, we hear a shriek from below while trotting over a bridge. It's a girl who has fallen into the drink. "Go ahead," Krish says, so I stick my head through the railing. A crowd has gathered on the bank below, people point at a figure swirling lazily in the current.

The water looks cold and deep—do I even know how to swim? I pretend I can't fit through the railings, I grunt and bark and strain. Krish can tell it's a show, since my body is so emaciated, it could pass through a slit. He shakes his head. "If you won't, I will," he says, and jumps in.

The current is faster than he thinks. He gets to the girl, even manages to clamp on to her dress. But then the river sweeps the two of them away. I come across his lifeless body as I race along the bank. He has a piece of fabric clamped between his teeth, the girl lies bloated next to him.

After that, it takes me many days to live down my shame. Also my disappointment, since surely Krish has graduated to a human being. How silly of me to fret about my own safety. I would have been fast-tracked into my next life—so efficient to be killed. Just as I'm despairing, though, another opportunity appears.

The boy has headphones on, and is busy texting something. He's about to step onto the crosswalk, so I bark at him. But he keeps going—doesn't he see the truck bearing down on him?

I charge into the street and snap at his feet. Startled, he falls backwards, out of harm's way. The truck swerves wildly and crashes into a nearby building.

A crowd gathers around us. I expected to be flattened, but I've escaped with only some bruises. A woman wraps me in a blanket and calls me a hero. A postman tickles me under the ear, I'm cooed over by a group of giggling children. I'm even petted by the boy I saved.

Suddenly, the driver of the crashed truck runs screaming towards us. "It's going to blow," he says, and I have just enough time to notice that the truck is actually a tanker. Then the explosion comes, so strong, it blows half the building away.

I'm instantly worried about the minus points I'll earn in case anyone has perished. Thankfully, the driver has survived, the people around me look fine. The children are crying, but they all seem to be safe.

I try to comfort the child next to me by licking its face. It closes its eyes and stops crying, then gurgles a bit. To my shock, its features abruptly begin to dissolve like in a horror comic. Bits of cheek come up with each lick.

I turn to the woman, and she is clutching in surprise at her chest. Her nose slides into her mouth, she begins to decompose before my eyes. The truck driver, the postman, the rest of the onlookers, all seem similarly afflicted.

I run from the scene. Cars crash into each other all around, people melt to the ground, always with that look of horrible surprise. I keep running until the night blots out the gory sights.

It's now a week since the accident took place. Apparently, the building was a medical research lab, the explosion let something deadly escape. Dogs are immune, I gather, but it might be curtains for the human race.

As I wander through the desolate streets, I wonder what Krish would say. Does it make sense to want to be a man if mankind no longer exists? For me, it probably doesn't matter—I should try to enjoy this existence, no matter how grim. Who knows how many lifetimes before I rise to a dog again?

——————

MANIL SURI, the Indian-American author of *The Death of Vishnu* and *The Age of Shiva,* is a mathematics professor at the University of Maryland, Baltimore County. His new novel is *The City of Devi.*

Daniel Torday

1. It was originally spelled with two *n*'s. It rhymes with Bonn. At Ellis Island they cut the second *n*. No one knows why.

2. All happy families might be happy in the same way—but the Mans were either wholly elatedly manically happy, or depressed. Every single Man. There's not one Man we can think of who has a middle ground.

3. Well, there was Uncle Torvald.

4. No one liked Uncle Torvald. Never got invited to weddings or bar mitzvahs, stood in back among the friends at funerals. Uncle Torvald was so even-keeled. You'd be hard-pressed to find a Man in the Greater Boston Area with a kind word for Torvald Man.

5. After the fourth beer, talking politics at the dinner table is not a good idea. Especially with old middle-of-the-road Uncle Torvald. That guy would even-keel you into throwing a punch every time. Depressed or happy as you may be. You say pro-life or pro-gun and he'll start preaching empathy. Say pro-choice and he'll start quoting Leviticus. Don't even think the word "adultery." Uncle Torvald was so even-keeled, he could get you to think adultery was okay.

6. In #5 above, the same is true if you say "Old Fashioned" or "Manhattan" or "Moscow Mule" instead of "beer."

7. There was the time Uncle Torvald took up with Aunt Lucia at Hyman Mann's wedding. Hyman being the one Man who'd

reclaimed the second *n*. And there was Uncle Torvald going after his own cousin's wife.

8. Maybe Uncle Torvald didn't know Aunt Lucia was Uncle Shy's wife.

9. Maybe Uncle Torvald had forgotten Uncle Shy had gone quadriplegic since the Diving Board Incident in Bubby's backyard pool.

10. If Uncle Torvald had been manic at the time, maybe he could have even been forgiven.

11. Or depressed.

12. When we found him in the Hilton bathroom with his Jockeys touching the tile floor and Aunt Lucia looking up at us like she was some kind of innocent—there are no innocent Mans—we had no choice but to take Uncle Torvald out in the parking lot and show him what it is to be a Man.

13. The fifth beer has essentially the same effect as the fourth.

14. In #5, you could replace the word "beer" with "gin Gibson" or "Manischewitz" or "meeting with Aunt Lucia."

15. Oh man we hated Uncle Torvald.

16. Sometimes they'll say a Jew isn't tough. If they say that, bring them to us.

17. They sure haven't met Uncle Torvald. He survived the Parking Lot Beating. And that's saying something. There were bricks that night, after all. Broken bottles.

18. He stopped that Aunt Lucia *mishigas* though.

19. And here's the one thing you can say about Uncle Torvald: He didn't even hold a grudge. He saw the other side. Empathy. That's what I mean about even-keeling you straight under the table. That's not how to be a Man. Not of the Greater Boston Area Mans, it's not.

20. So just think: What would Uncle Torvald do? And then do the opposite. Or better yet, don't think at all.

21. Man. Two *n*'s. Like a Jamaican would say it, or a German. Man.

Daniel Torday, director of creative writing at Bryn Mawr, is the author of the short novel *The Sensualist*, winner of the 2012 National Jewish Book Awards' Goldberg Prize for Outstanding Debut Fiction.

Monique Truong

She walked around me three times. Each revolution took about half an hour. On the first pass, I saw black waterproof boots and pants. Second pass, a bright orange parka, hood up. The silver zipper that kept the garment closed went past her neck and up to the bridge of her nose. I saw only her eyes, but I knew she wasn't the one.

She was the first of the team to arrive. Eventually, thirty more would come, running towards me like I was going somewhere. I've failed to note their sex. They're moving too quickly, their eyes blurred and narrowed against the blowing sand. I'm not certain how long "eventually" means now, but we had about an hour together. She orbiting me like a moon, you might think, but I was the moon and she the astronaut, airlocked.

She made multiple phone calls during our time together: "Setsu, here." She was so breathless. "Emaciated but no visible wounds," she reported.

Am pleased to meet you, Setsu. I'm twenty years old. I'm male. Perhaps you'll name me, when this is over.

Setsu jumped in place to keep warm, her orange torso, lifting and falling, against the stippled gray sky. The sight of this made me warm, and I fell asleep.

"I've called Coastal Studies. My supervisor is rounding up the team. Christ, I can't believe this is happening. *This* is really happening on my freakin' first week," Setsu was screaming into the phone when I awoke.

Setsu really likes to talk on the phone.

Setsu is afraid to be alone with me. This one wasn't a thought; it was a sense, like the changing temperature of water.

"I've gotta go, Josh. I've gotta go. I think there's movement."

Setsu tucked her phone into a front pocket of her parka. She reached out to touch the side of my head then pulled back her hand, almost slapping it with her other one.

She took the phone back out and photographed me instead.

Phone-camera, water-repellent fabric, the brown edged in blue of Setsu's eyes. I like it here.

Inch by inch, she was attempting to document me. Am I going somewhere, Setsu?

Setsu is a scientist.

Setsu is the color orange.

I can't decide which fact I liked more.

Setsu isn't the one, but she is the one now. I'm twenty years old, and I'm male. *Now* is what I should want.

Setsu jumps in place, but she's really not the one.

Setsu will find the other photographs and the report, a list of the unanswered questions in the files.

It was about four miles up the coast. I knew what I was doing this time. If I'd misjudged and gone too far south I would have been in some other group's jurisdiction, the Riverhead Foundation maybe. Coastal Studies was what her orange parka had said, and like an unsatisfied customer I had come back to lodge my complaint.

The team arrived and slipped a pad underneath my belly. Strapped a corsetlike ring around my lower body and pulled me backwards into the incoming tide. By the end, there were television cameras. There were reporters. They all repeated these words like they were praying: "A new rescue method."

She, the first one, had been by my side. The entire time, her body was humming. Though I was much stronger that time, I became weak when I heard her. The bargelike boat that was doing most of the work met little resistance then. Despite the low frequency pulses coming from her body, which lulled me with her "I will, I will, I will," she waded back to shore, clapping and cheering with the others as I disappeared from view.

An ocean was not deep enough to hold my disappointment, my anger, my ache.

This past summer I saw my brother near the Gulf of Mexico. He said that this weakness ran in our family. Our father on Breezy Point. Our uncle on Pittenweem. Two months ago, my brother joined the list. He chose the south shore of St. Croix.

Setsu's body wasn't humming, but nor was it silent. Before they arrived and swarmed us both, she began to cry. She sat herself down on the sand, steps away from my eye, as if she knew.

MONIQUE TRUONG is a Vietnamese-American author of *The Book of Salt* and, most recently, *Bitter in the Mouth*.

Luis Alberto Urrea

——————

They wore their best clothes and waited for the Old Man. Billy didn't own a suit, but he'd found a tie somewhere. He stood at the window, watching the Old Man water the garden.

His sister said, "What's he doing now?"

"Wait."

"We're going to be late."

"Just … wait."

She looked at her husband in the living room and shook her head. The Old Man, Mr. Iron Fist, loved drunken Billy the most. She sighed. Well, at least Billy'd cut his hair.

"He's getting dirty," she said.

Billy watched Pops shuffle in the dirt, mud on his brogans and dirt on his cuffs. That brown suit had to be fifty years old. But the fedora was stylin'. He smiled.

"I need a smoke," he said. His sister didn't smoke. "Start the car. I'll fetch him."

He stepped out of the gloom into a bright cube of light and leaves and butterflies. Good stink of fresh mud. He lit up. Pops watered his apple tree.

"Getting late, Pops," he said.

The Old Man turned off the spigot.

"Sonny," he said. "We planted this tree the day you were born." He'd told this to Billy a thousand times.

Billy pulled out his handkerchief.

"You got mud on your shoes."

Pops braced himself on his kneeling son's shoulder as Billy cleaned his feet.

"Is it terrible, Billy?" he asked.

Billy led him around to the front. Pops paused and bent to the raised carnation beds. He plucked one and sniffed it.

"Mother's favorite," he said.

Billy tossed his smoke.

"It's not bad, Pops. Not too bad. She looks like she's asleep."

The car was waiting.

"Is it okay?" the Old Man asked. "I drop this flower in with her?"

Billy took his elbow. His arm felt like little sticks. The sidewalk was broken up out here. Uneven.

"It's okay, Pops. I promise."

Sis opened the door.

Pops tipped his hat to her and climbed in.

Luis Alberto Urrea is a Mexican-American novelist and poet. His nonfiction book *The Devil's Highway* was a finalist for the Pulitzer Prize in 2005. His most recent novel is *Queen of America*.

Juan Gabriel Vásquez

To the right, beyond the sliding doors, is the waiting room: a square fish tank full of low armchairs, their orange fabric worn threadbare by years of friction from impatient bodies. Coming in, Javier is glad not to recognize anyone; he sits down under the TV mounted on the wall like a vigilant eye, and is about to start a fictitious conversation on his cell phone, just to feel less awkward, when he sees Ricardo Rocha crossing the hallway with a doctor. "No news yet," he says. "Nothing to do but wait." Javier watches Ricardo walk up to him, stretch out his hand, and then, changing his mind, spread his arms wide to embrace him. This indecision is perturbing. But there's no sense in worrying: Ricardo can't possibly know. The location, Ricardo says, is all they know about the accident: a sharp bend on a mountain road, halfway between the highlands of Bogotá and the sweltering Magdalena Valley. In some versions, Guadalupe's motorbike skids on loose stones, the remains of a recent landslide; in others, she tries to overtake a brown tractor-trailer when she shouldn't have. But everybody agrees that she attempted an emergency maneuver, and witnesses saw her skidding on the hot blacktop, hanging on to the bike and sliding, like a fallen ballerina, until her body crashed into one of those painted rocks that locals use as tombstones. It seemed miraculous that the blow to her head didn't kill her on the spot. Now a hole has been drilled in her skull to drain the blood.

Javier listens to all this with keen sympathy, as you listen to a childhood friend. But his mind is elsewhere: in Guadalupe's white-tiled hospital room, watching her unequal struggle against death. Ricardo speaks about her body, her left kneecap displaced by the impact, the pale skin of her left arm torn in places, half her face darkened to that purple tone, so dark it's almost black. He talks about the strands of hair stuck to the inside of the helmet; he talks about the helmet itself, its dent that changed color, just like Guadalupe's face.

When exactly does the transformation begin? When does Javier realize, not without some trepidation, that the past is changing in Guadalupe's absence? Later he will try to determine it like a traveler looking at a map after finally finding his way: slowly, hesitantly, Javier is entering a new life, as if he has just been forgiven: he who has no right to forgiveness, he whose deeds are beyond the absolution of his fellow men. In the waiting room, alone in the company of strangers, Javier considers a world in which nobody else knows, and thus a world in which he has no longer done what he did, a world in which he will be—the mere idea is an impertinence, a provocation—a new man.

———

Colombian writer JUAN GABRIEL VÁSQUEZ is the author of *The Informers*. His new novel is *The Sound of Things Falling*.

Daniel Wallace

I remember the old man perched in his second-story window, milky behind the wavy glass, glaring at all us kids like we were the mice and he was the hungry hawk. We played in his yard sometimes. I never met him. I thought—in my nightmares—that one day he'd pitch himself through the window and grab one of us, hold us in his arms until we crumbled, sucking our life out through his withered chicken-skinned body and dragging himself back inside, appearing at the window again, waiting for another one of us to drift into his gaze, living forever. He didn't live, though: One day he died. It happened the way it happens when you're young: On a different plane, like clouds. I just remember wearing the coat and tie I never wore, the shoes so tight, my toes bled, in a church we never went to, surrounded by the smell of the strange and old. We went back to his house after, and I went inside for the first time. His wife shivered in a big green chair, not even crying: I think she was all dried up. I ate a little sandwich, then I went outside to see if he was still there at the window—and he was. I knew he would be. He waved, all friendly, and I waved back, I don't know why. My throat felt strangled. Then he disappeared, fading back into the dark, and I never saw him there again. I didn't tell anybody. I didn't know what it meant, because even that young I knew I didn't believe in anything. I told my wife about it, though, twenty years later. We were in bed in the dark. The story scared her, but not the way it had scared me. *We're only as gone as we want to be,* she said, *that's what that means,* and she cried because she never wanted to think that this—all of this, our brand-new world together—wasn't enough. *It means I can't love you forever,* she said, and she was right.

———

DANIEL WALLACE is the author of five novels, most notably *Big Fish,* which inspired Tim Burton's film of the same name. His most recent novel is *The Kings and Queens of Roam.*

Jess Walter

Oh that fucking Peter Pan hit-and-run cocksucker. Thoughtless asshole, selfish prick. Not that she should be surprised; Marcus was a bolter, a runner; he always left in the dark. "It's like dating Houdini," she used to tell her friends. Maggie could cuff him, straitjacket him, lock him in a steamer trunk, and at 3:00 A.M., the goddamn commitment-phobe would tiptoe out in the dark, belt undone, shoes in hand.

"Yeah, I'm not big on *good morning,*" he used to say, shorthand for I'm going to keep fucking other women.

No, it wasn't that she was surprised. Marcus was an immature, womanizing douchetool when they'd met three years ago. Which was okay then. After eighteen months of shotgun marriage, the last thing Maggie wanted was another lousy husband. But how could someone so happy with himself ever change?

No, honestly, what bothered her...was that it bothered her. She'd known just what she was getting last night. She'd wanted just this: to feel his weight, to lose herself. Marcus inside.

So why did waking up alone now make her feel like such a failure...as a feminist, or an existentialist...or what? Shouldn't it be enough to get laid? To smell him in the bed, see the indentation in the other pillow, think—Good fuck. Right. Move on.

Instead she felt empty and on the verge of tears, certain she would spend the rest of her life as a pathetic, bitter single mother—

bullshit cliché—her thoughts looping into a women's magazine quiz she'd taken during the whole Marcus breakup ("Will He Ever Commit?") and then, worst of all—to her mother's pet word, *used*. Of all the fucking words. No one had used anyone; why did she feel fucked and put away? She had the urge to sue someone, her mom, or Marcus, or those girls from eighth grade, or the Catholic Church, maybe a class-action suit against the makers of that word, *used*.

Maybe it was just time and place, the circumstances that made her feel so awful, the shock of seeing him last night for the first time in six months, having him show up at the wake like that. ("Your dad would've hated that I was here, huh?") Marcus looked great in a suit, my God, those cyclist's shoulders and hips; then the Jameson started flowing and the stories, and it was nice to laugh and Marcus half apologized for not calling for so long and even if it was bullshit, it was... nice, and when they were walking to their cars she practically willed him to say something, anything, so when he looked over in the parking lot and said, simply, "Well...," that was all it took; she was helpless, incapable of coming up with a pro/con list... or a thought, because at that moment there were only two things in the universe: alone and Marcus. And last night she could not do alone.

Maggie sat up in bed. She looked down at her breasts. Was there any lasting benefit from something like last night, any residue? It had been six months since she'd had sex and now it had been six hours. But did being touched have any weight the next day, any value? It wasn't like she could feel his hands anymore, like she could feel anything. Except sadness. A yawning sense of alone. Maggie opened her nightstand for some Advil and that's when she noticed, in the corner, on the floor behind the bathroom door, in a heap, a gray suit jacket.

She heard faint voices then, from the kitchen. She got out of bed, pulled her robe on, and went downstairs.

In the kitchen Dustin stood on a chair across from Marcus. They were eye to eye, each holding neckties. They were a foot apart, shirtless, and they had the ties looped around their bare necks. Marcus was in his boxer shorts, Dustin in his Transformer pajama pants.

"Do what I do," Marcus said. "Like looking in a mirror."

Shoulder blades jutted from Dustin's tiny pale back.

"Cross the woods," Marcus said.

"Cross the woods," Dustin said.

"Over the hill," Marcus said.

"Over," Dustin said.

"Around."

"Around."

"Behind."

"Behind."

"And through."

"Through."

"Perfect. Now turn around and show your mom," Marcus said.

Dustin turned. He beamed, surprised to see his mother in the doorway. "Look," he said, "I'm wearing Grandpa's tie."

The tie was blue, with little red sailing flags. It hung past Dustin's feet. He must've gotten it out of the box in the living room that Maggie's stepmother sent home with her. It was looped in the sort of unmanageable knot Dustin always got in his sneakers.

Maggie wondered then if there wasn't just one ache in the world: sad, happy, horny, drunk, sorry, satisfied, grieving, lonely. If we believed these to be different feelings but they all came from the same sweet unbearable spring.

Marcus had made coffee. He handed her a cup. She put it to her lips until she could speak again. Finally, she said to her son, in a half whisper, "It looks so good on you, baby."

JESS WALTER is the author of, most recently, *Beautiful Ruins* and the short story collection *We Live in Water*.

Josh Weil

The boys—men, now, he supposes—lift whips, stare into the women's eyes, and, with all their field-plowing, machete-chopping strength, let loose. The crack of splitting skin. Bright wet bloodstripes in the sun.

Some backs are netted with thumb-thick welts, wounds lumpy from paste rubbed in to make them rise, and he remembers the guide telling him the chant—*we give you our blood, we give you our blood*—though he can hardly hear it over the blaring horns, the ankle bells. The women stomp them loud, choose a man from among the throng, draw him by his wrist, insist on being whipped, staring into his eyes, blowing hornblasts at his face, till he gives in. To his sister? His mother? His wife?

Which one, he wonders, will the bull jumper choose? Earlier he'd asked, *And if he falls?* The guide had slugged back fermented sorghum slush. *Then he waits another year before he can try again to make a marriage.* That is what he has come to see: the boy stripped naked, slathered with grease, gleaming in the setting sun, running towards the line of twenty bulls, leaping onto their backs, shifting spine to shifting spine, while all the others chant, beat hands, urge him on towards the moment when, vaulting off of the last bull, he'll be a man.

How his wife would have loved to see it. Lectures at the Explorers Club, exhibits in the Africa wing: In the last months she was ceaselessly leaving for the city. Saturday morning he might wake to her flute practice, slip out for a jog, return to the hush of air-conditioning around his too-loud breath. Sunday he'd glance through a window—her, outside, planting tomato starts—pass by again a little later: the black tray a hole in the grass, the trowel a glint she'd left. Friday nights, home from work, he'd idle in the driveway, watching the garage door rise, chest hollowing with each inch of emptiness exposed. Sometime after the last time, after the weeks haunting the city hoping for a glimpse of her, after the late trains home with his face turned from all the other commuters pretending they didn't know, after night after night of watching YouTube clips she'd left in his browser's history—a man hacking through a jungle, a woman prying a lip plate from her mouth, a boy running across the backs of bulls—he had begun to see them in his dreams: bare black feet slamming spine to spine to the backbone he knew from the thousand times he'd run his fingers down it; fingers stretching her lip around a disk, the rip of skin, her bloody teeth. One morning he tore up the tomato plants. Another, he took her flute to the garage, unlatched the toolbox, sat in her abandoned spot, prying off buttons, pounding the silver tube flat.

The shaking ground, the pounding feet. Now they are blowing their horns at him. In his hand: a whip, pressed there by a boy who grins, teeth white as his painted face. On his own cheeks the dried daubs pinch; earlier, the guide had urged him to accept the stippling, said it would be rude not to join in. But now? This? The guide won't even meet his eyes. The women hold their gazes on anything but his.

His is on her: there, at a table by a window, tearing at a bit of naan. He'd stood on the sidewalk, the evening rush breaking around him. She'd seen him—the morsel falling, her fingers going to her face, her eyes filling with a fear as if she thought he'd come straight through the glass, thought him capable of something terrible. *It's me,* he said. She rose—on her cheek her fingertips had left faint marks of grease—and turned—they caught the light—and fled.

The bells grow louder. The ground shakes. The air reeks of rancid fat. Before him a woman stamp-dances closer, her body smeared with gleam, until she's near enough he sees the welt wrapping one cheek, unfolding in a bloom of flesh where an eye should be. In his fist the switch is the other end of that stem, that scar the tip of his whip.

We give you our blood, the woman chants, and it is only then that he realizes she is talking to someone behind him. Turning, he sees the impatient stare, the boy waiting for him to get out of the way. Somewhere, he knows, the bull jumper is waiting, too. Somewhere, his wife is sitting at a table, alone, unwatched, at peace. Beneath him, the ground goes unsteady. He tries to stand still. Behind him, the women stamp. The bells jangle. He stands. *We give you our blood.* The man raises the whip.

JOSH WEIL's debut collection of novellas, *The New Valley,* won the Sue Kaufman Award for first fiction. His next book, *The Great Glass Sea,* will be published next spring.

Terry Tempest Williams

I

"By God, no brother of mine is going to die on the factory floor," he said to the men around him. "Goddammit, help me."

II

"He's not a dog," the man said to his wife as they were driving home late at night.

"He's a little boy in a brown dog suit." The dog-boy turned to the woman and snarled a grin.

III

"Forgive me," he wrote to his daughter and then lit another cigarette. There, he had said it, no need to mail the letter.

IV

"Gentlemen, I appreciate the fact that my daughters brought you to the house to talk to me about moving to the retirement home. Your presentation was impressive, but I'm not going anywhere."

He snapped a match off his fingernail.

A week later he died in his own bed and was buried with his radio.

V

"I said I don't want to talk about it—"

TERRY TEMPEST WILLIAMS is the author of *When Women Were Birds* and *Finding Beauty in a Broken World*, among many others.

John Wray

My troubles began this way: I followed a little blond-haired girl into the park. It had been a long, brutal winter and I'd spent my time hiding under bridges, re-creating key scenes from my childhood. Food was scarce, firewood nonexistent. My memories, therefore, of my youth, and of the way things had been "different" in those golden, breezy days, were my sole source of heat during those icy months. Images returned to me, zoetrope-like, as I crouched in the dark with my bloody ax handle, waiting for something worth bludgeoning to pass under the bridge. How tired the world seemed compared with the liveliness and gumption of those infinitely tender auld lang syne!

The year electricity was invented, for example, my brothers and I were so dirty we broke knives trying to clean under our fingernails. Father brought home bigger and bigger trophies to impress us with, culminating in this anvil I'm now chained to. Mother wasn't at home much, being in the Register. From the start it was clear that something was "off" about me. There was even talk that I might be in the Register myself. I tried my best, God knows, to lose myself in my brothers' games, to take part in their pissing contests and to pull my plum contentedly with them round a plate of butter cookies (eating them afterwards, if my number came up, with a good-natured guffaw); nevertheless, family life wasn't for me. I pined for the green, rectilinear, semi-enclosed spaces of the suburbs. I yearned for the promenades and pastures of the park.

With time my brothers became strangers to me and I, for my part, barely recognized them. They were keeping tabs on me, though, you can bet; and when, on one especially fine autumn day—after years of keeping the family books in tip-top condition and sweeping up after their escapades and leaving the house before sunrise every morning for the bridges and back alleys of town and never ever coming back empty-handed when I could possibly help it—when, after all that, I finally made up my mind to follow a little blond-haired girl—with braids—into the park, they were on top of me in two seconds flat. "We've got you by the underpants, Johnny," they hissed, and I couldn't deny it. After the briefest of struggles they dragged me home and chained me to this anvil. There were so many of them that I lost count completely. Father was somewhere among the crowd, I knew, sniggering and rattling his jewelry. Mother certainly wasn't, as she's in the Register. Before I knew it I'd become a man.

JOHN WRAY is the author of *The Right Hand of Sleep*, *Canaan's Tongue*, and most recently, *Lowboy*.

Tiphanie Yanique

I found the video. It was in a white case. My father and me, we'd watched every kung fu movie he owned. Our favorite was *The Last Dragon*. He loved it because the main character was a strong black man. I loved it because my mother said the main character looked like me.

I'd told my parents that while they were out I'd watch the game. But then home alone, I'd kneeled to the library of kung fu and found an unmarked video I hadn't yet seen.

I popped two bags of extra butter popcorn in the microwave. I pulled my dad's chair up close to the TV. I inched the video to the lip of the machine until it was sucked in.

There were no opening credits. Just the words BIG MOMMA. The text written on a piece of paper and held up to the camera. Worse than a high school video project. I could hear a woman scolding. When the sign came down, there was my own naked mother.

She was lying on the bed with her legs spread open. She was young, almost as young, maybe, as I was. She had an afro on her head and one between her legs. She was thinner than I'd ever seen her.

I kept eating the popcorn. I was shoveling entire fistfuls into my mouth. Somehow I needed to finish these bags of popcorn.

Then there was her voice directed at the camera: "Come here, big boy." Then there was my dad. Lean and tall. Like me. His own afro like a devil's halo around his head as he climbed on top. Just like that. Her thighs cradling his hips. His chest leaning down to meet her breasts.

I wish I could say that I gnarled the video out of the machine. Or that I threw my popcorn in the air and ran from the room. But there was only the sensation that the woman, my mother, was beautiful and sexy and that my dick was stiff as stone. Maybe desire is an instinctive thing. I don't know. I just sat in the chair, leaning forward. Devouring popcorn like I was on a timer. If I got to the end of the popcorn then I would turn off the video. Something like that.

I can't say what this means about me, but the truth is I felt like I understood what people meant when they said you ended up marrying your mother. That woman in the video would have been my girlfriend, maybe.

Now she climbed on top of my father. From the camera's view I could see his whole self slipping and sliding in. The noises they made, unlike any kung fu flick. The things they said.

When the popcorn was down to kernels I set it aside. Both of them were facing away from me. She was on her hands and knees and his back was to me, his ass tensing and relaxing. I forced my penis through the zipper in my pants.

"Come on now," she said. "I'll be sore." From the profile I could see her face bunched up. I felt suddenly protective of her. I thought, he should stop. *I* would stop if I were him. Then my mother turned her head to look back at the camera directly. I came, without any coercion, into my fist.

Then his voice. "Now you know, I don't like to be rushed."

But he released himself from her and I breathed. Relieved it was all finally over. Until he turned towards the camera, his face no different than mine, and kneeled her down between his legs. He held the back of her head just like I'd imagined.

When I heard the garage door open I knew I didn't have a second of time. My mother usually got out of the car first and made her way to the door, hating the funk of the garage smell. "Man smell," my father always said, slapping me on the back. Though I hated the smell, too. Now I leapt at the VHS player and finally, Lord, finally, had the appropriate feeling of nausea. The tape took its gentle time ejecting. I grabbed it and its unmarked case. The slick from my hands spreading all over. I ran to my room, my zipper still down, and slammed my door. I turned widely around. I knew that the discovery of this would most definitely make me run away from home. I stuffed it under my pillow, and then after I'd taken a shower I hid it away in a shoe box. That was years ago. I've had the video ever since.

TIPHANIE YANIQUE is the author of *How to Escape from a Leper Colony*. She was named one of the National Book Foundation's 5 Under 35.

Mario Alberto Zambrano

Papi would come home from work with black stains over his shirt. I remember him washing his hands at the kitchen sink, scrubbing his knuckles in front of the window. He stopped doing it after a while and I got used to his hands looking like he'd been working under the hood of a car.

He came home one day wearing a smile that looked like he'd been given an award. He'd been given a promotion as managing director of inventory planning, which sounded better than steelworker. Mom told us later when she was tucking us in that he was going to be assigned to the second floor with a window in his office. The next morning we were going shopping to buy him a suit and a briefcase.

There was one time Papi was watching TV and Mom and Estrella had gone to the supermarket. It was just the two of us and I asked him what he would've wanted to be if he would've gone to school. He said he wanted to be a painter. Not of houses, but an artist. In the garage, there was a painting of his of a waterfall between two mountains and two deer. When we'd clean the garage or take down Christmas decorations from the attic, I'd stare at it. And I never could believe Papi had painted it because it looked so professional.

He was in the dressing room at Mervyn's trying on a navy blue suit for his new promotion and it was like he'd stepped out of

a movie. "Where's the sombrero?" I joked. I wanted him to sing. I
wanted him to do a two-step. I extended my arms and said, "¡Ay!
Te ves muy caballero." Estrella brought him ties of different colors
and told him how smart he looked. He'd put them on as he wig-
gled his toes under his socks, then stand in front of the mirror
wearing his silly smile. Our faces would peek out from the sides
of his back checking to see what a managing director looked like.

That night Papi kept grabbing a section of the newspaper even
though he'd already looked through it. He'd walk to the garage
and come back again. Before I went to bed I gave him a hug.

"¿Qué?" he said. "You never do that."

When I got home from school the following day Mom called.
"He didn't get it," she said. Just like that. Like if he'd forgotten
to pick up cereal on his way home.

"What?"

"He didn't get it, Luz."

She was on the other side of the interstate helping someone put
together a piñata for a posada the following weekend. She wasn't
getting home until later and said it didn't work out because they
changed their minds. Maybe it was his English. She didn't know.
"Just be nice. Don't say anything. Act normal." I hung up knowing that at any minute he'd walk through the door, and I didn't
know what to do. I thought of going to Tencha's to help her with
tamales, but I went to my room instead. When he came home I
pretended to be asleep.

That weekend when we played Lotería with the Silvas, Papi
did something he'd never done before. When you call the cards
to play the game you sing the riddles. That's what makes it different from American bingo. It's not as easy as calling out numbers because in Lotería you have to figure out the riddle that'll
reveal the card. Either that or keep your eyes on the cards being
thrown. But the faster the riddles, the faster the game.

Papi got up and dealt the cards. At first his voice was off-key, and you could tell he was nervous. But he got stronger the more we played.

Don Ferruco en la alameda, su bastón quería tirar!—(El Catrín)
Para el sol y para el agua!—(El Paraguas)
El que con la cola pica, le dan una paliza!—(El Alácran)

Everyone knows these riddles from church fairs and parties. But there's some that people make up for fun. Like *La Sirena*. Tío Fernando would whistle when she was called because she's topless, and Pancho Silva, who normally dealt the cards, would say, "*La encuerada para tu Tío Fernando!*" For *El Venado: "Lo que tu Tío José mata cada fin de semana!*"

But the day Papi dealt, I hadn't known he knew the riddles because I'd never heard him deal, just like I'd never known he wanted to be a painter.

He started singing the riddles and they sounded like songs he'd learned from when he was a boy. I couldn't keep up with the game because he was singing so fast, so loud. Pancho kept bringing him beers, raising his volume. I looked at Papi, with his chin up and his heart so open and unafraid of what people thought of him. I sat there and looked at him and didn't even try to play, because I couldn't. In my head I started to clap, softly at first, then louder and louder until someone called out with such a burst of enthusiasm it brought laughter to the table: *¡Lotería!*

Mexican-American MARIO ALBERTO ZAMBRANO is a former contemporary ballet dancer turned novelist. His debut novel, *Lotería*, was published in July.

About the Editors

Colum McCann, a cofounder of Narrative 4 and contributing editor at *Esquire,* is the National Book Award–winning author of *Let the Great World Spin.* His new novel is *TransAtlantic.*

Tyler Cabot is the articles and fiction editor of *Esquire,* where he's worked since 2003.

Lisa Consiglio has developed and led nonprofits for over twenty years and is a cofounder of Narrative 4.

About *Esquire*

Esquire, published by Hearst Magazines, is a general-interest magazine for men. Founded in 1933, *Esquire* offers pieces on diverse topics from politics and sports to fashion and the arts. The magazine has always been a showcase for fiction, including F. Scott Fitzgerald and Ernest Hemingway in its early days, Cormac McCarthy and David Foster Wallace in the 1990s, and Stephen King and Colum McCann today.

Esquire is the most honored monthly magazine in America, with a total of sixteen National Magazine Awards over the past fifteen years. In addition to its U.S. flagship edition, *Esquire* publishes twenty-six editions around the world.

About NARRATIVE4
Moving Stories

Narrative 4 was founded by a group of authors and activists who believe something as simple as a story can change the world. We connect people and communities everywhere through the sharing of stories and are working to create a global narrative for all of us.

Although storytelling is an ancient and universal human activity, Narrative 4 gives people all over the world the ability to share their stories in a new and powerful way. We identify those globally who may otherwise be voiceless—whether it be teens from the South Side of Chicago, young women in Kabul, highschoolers in Newtown, Connecticut, or the disenfranchised in Lagos, Nigeria—and bring them to a safe space to tell a significant story from their lives. They are then given the chance to own and articulate someone else's story—to craft it and carry it with them back to their communities. These story exchanges build a mutual trust that strips away the typical narratives of cynicism and despair, allowing new ones to take shape: A narrative for immigration. A narrative for the environment. A narrative for religion. A narrative for peace. And on and on.

We invite you to join us and become a part of our narrative. Our members have the opportunity to learn about upcoming story exchanges, meet the N4 students, advisors, and local partners, and discover what our authors are currently writing and reading. Together, we are moving stories.

Narrative 4 is a project of the Tides Center. For more information or to help, please visit Narrative4.com.

3 1170 00945 3667